THIS MESSY
MOBILE LIFE

· ·

HOW A MOLA CAN HELP
GLOBALLY MOBILE FAMILIES
CREATE A LIFE BY DESIGN

Mariam Navaid Ottimofiore

"Every now and then, a book comes along that leapfrogs ahead of others on similar topics. Mariam Navaid Ottimofiore's accessible, engaging and thorough *This Messy Mobile Life IS* that book. No matter who or where you on your cross-cultural journey, you will be able to tease out strands (or chunks) of your own messy, mobile, multiple-multi, MOLA life in its pages. Simply stunning."

Linda A. Janssen
Author of *The Emotionally Resilient Expat:
Engage, Adapt and Thrive Across Cultures*

o o o

"Family members are unique when looked at in isolation but when the family unit is woven together it represents acceptance, tolerance, and unity. Ottimofiore's MOLA is a great example of this. Having a technique for mixing multicultural identities and the permission to know that not everything needs to be equal to create a beautiful family tapestry is priceless."

Julia Simens
Author of *Emotional Resilience and the Expat Child: Practical tips and
storytelling techniques that will strengthen the global family*

o o o

"Mariam boldly addresses the challenges and complexities that come with being a globally mobile family. Armed with insight, expertise, and practical methodology, Mariam has untangled what can seem daunting and guides us through the process of sculpting the beauty of an international, cross-cultural, multilingual lifestyle more and more people are embracing."

Christopher O'Shaughnessy
International Speaker and author of
Arrival, Departures and the Adventures In-Between

o o o

"In This Messy Mobile Life Mariam invites us to step into the space where chaos can turn into order and upheaval into beauty. This book reminds globally mobile and culturally diverse families that we can create an amazing MOLA of life from the many layers of ourselves we call home."

Jodi Harris
Expat Coach and Mindfulness Teacher at
World Tree Coaching, LLC and co-author of *Kids on the Move: 25 Activities to help kids connect, reflect and thrive around the world*
www.worldtreecoaching.com

o o o

"A brilliant untangling of the complex situations and perspectives that multicultural families face. A blueprint for mobile families to transform a mess of cultural identities into a masterpiece."

Lisa Ferland
Author of *Knocked Up Abroad*

o o o

"This Messy Mobile Life beautifully weaves together story and instruction, giving us a remarkable tool for the global journey. Mariam's voice emerges as authentic, wise, and strong as she speaks into this complicated yet extraordinary expat/TCK life. This book will soon be on the shelves of expats and third culture kids around the world, as well it should be."

Marilyn R. Gardner
Author of *Between Worlds, Essays on Culture & Belonging & Worlds Apart: A Third Culture Kid's Journey*

o o o

"Mariam shares the beautiful story of her multicultural, multilingual, globally mobile family in her engaging writing style and gives tools to readers through her MOLA framework to transform a possible mess into a beautiful design to own, personalize and wear with pride. Her advice is supported by research, enriched with stories from other global families and addresses real-life scenarios. Highly recommend this book to everyone who lives a globally mobile life or supports those who do."

Tamania Jafri
TEDx Speaker on Language and Identity and Writer at UrduMom.com

o o o

"This is a perfect and honest go-to book for globally mobile families filled with practical advice brought to you through the intimate stories of Mariam's family experiences. An inspiring guide on how a family can embrace the mobile life and thrive."

Kristine Racina
Executive Director, The Expatriate Archive Centre

o o o

"This book is an incredibly extensive account of personal and theoretical content that helps families acknowledge and share the many strengths associated with their complex international lifestyle. I love that Mariam gives us this term 'mola' to talk about all that it entails, and this book really is for EVERYONE with the countless examples that will allow anyone to 'see themselves' in what's written. The insights and the reflection activities will be welcomed for parents who are looking for ways they can support their kids in the midst of relocation. Mariam has positioned herself right there amongst some of the top experts in the field with this work."

Kate Berger MSc
Child Psychologist and Founder of The Expat Kids Club

o o o

"This Messy Mobile Life is a wonderfully welcome addition to the mobile, cross-cultural and ethnically diverse community. Mariam honors one of the TCK 'tribal elders', Norma McCaig, deftly adapting the Mola layered art-form into an image and a tool for adaptation and integration. Increasing family complexity meets powerful resource!"

Michael V. Pollock
Director of Interaction International, Founder of
Daraja TCK, International Educator, Co-Author of
Third Culture Kids: Growing Up Among Worlds 3rd Ed

*To Norma McCaig for first introducing the
mola as a metaphor for living a globally rich life,*

and

*To Martino, Mina and Mikail for helping me
make our beautiful MOLA Family.*

ACKNOWLEDGMENTS

I would like to thank many people for their help with this book. First and foremost, my loving husband, Martino, for allowing me to share so honestly our own trials and tribulations in paving the way through our rather messy global lives. Thank you for being my biggest supporter and sparring partner as I brought this book to life. My kids, Mina and Mikail, who suffered the consequences of the hours I spent at my laptop and wondered out loud, "Why is Mama never finished?" And my extended family: my parents Nighat and Navaid, my parents-in-law Marlies and Salvatore and my sister Salma who offered support and unsolicited advice from different corners of the world. I love you all and probably would have finished this book much earlier had it not been for all your frequent questions which ironically did provide some of my best inspiration.

I'd like to thank my incredible editor, writing mentor and friend Jo Parfitt. Without her help, support and guidance, I would still be sitting in my garden procrastinating and wondering how to write this book. Thank you, Jo, for your excellent editorial advice and for meeting me in all corners of the world to write this book – from Dubai to The Hague and almost in Marrakech – and for Skyping with me across multiple time zones in Europe, Asia and Africa, even in countries where Skype was officially banned.

Without the help of my wonderful nine experts, Ruth Van Reken, Valérie Besanceney, Kristin Louise Duncombe, Sundae Schneider-Bean, Jerry Jones, Trisha Carter, Rita Rosenback, Ute Limacher-Riebold and Soile Pietikäinen, I could not have completed this book. I thank all of you for offering your expert advice on the challenges and solutions for living this messy, multicultural, multilingual and multi-mobile life.

A special thank you to Ruth for digging through old papers and helping me find Norma McCaig's early work on mola as a metaphor for living your best global life. I drew huge inspiration from Norma's work as the Founder of Global Nomads International, and her coining of the term 'global nomad', which we use so often today, inspired me to coin my own new term in this book 'MOLA Family.' And thank you to Robin Pascoe for making me do a victory dance in my living room by agreeing to write the foreword for this book. I can't think of anyone better than you to introduce this book!

I would like to thank every single respondent who took my **'Mobile Family Survey'** in 2018 to help with my research and understanding in charting out the challenges and opportunities faced by global families around the world. I would also like to thank the entire team at Summertime Publishing and Springtime Books who put the book together and offered timely support and advice related to editing, production and design, and thank you, Helena Jalanka, for creating my MOLA icon and design. And thank you to my husband's employer for inadvertently ensuring we made an international move in the middle of writing this book. It meant that while I was writing about a messy global life, I was also living through the mess on a daily basis.

Last but not least, I would like to thank the wonderfully loyal readers of my expat blog 'And Then We Moved To' for supporting me and my writing through our various adventures. Without so much online and offline support from my international tribe, this book would not have been possible.

Mariam Navaid Ottimofiore
Accra, Ghana, November 2018.

CONTENTS

FOREWORD

I first had the pleasure of watching Mariam in action at the 2018 Families in Global Transition conference in The Hague when she presented: "The 'Other' Expats: Diverse Voices from Dubai and How Race, Class and Privilege Affect our Mobility." Listening to her presentation, I truly understood her commitment to examining the diversity of the expatriate experience.

As part of her research, Mariam interviewed and recorded the opinions of migrant workers, many of them from her native Pakistan, who were working in Dubai and whose needs are typically marginalized or completely ignored. Mariam gave them a voice and underscored the notion that one size definitely does not fit all expats.

Now, with *This Messy Mobile Life* she has taken her commitment to inclusion to an entirely new level and provides a fresh, admirable voice to the challenges facing multicultural, multilingual families. Combining research with her own life stories, she provides a creative framework to help families like her own succeed.

Introducing the idea of a 'mola' – an intricately designed and richly complex South American textile which you will read about in the pages to follow – Mariam advises readers to not only embrace their own unique lives, but to proactively design them as well as she has done.

So many of the challenges of raising a family become magnified when transplanted to another country and multiculturalism is no exception. By addressing these in *This Messy Mobile Life*, Mariam has contributed an outstanding new addition to the global family literature.

Robin Pascoe
Director, Global Communications
– Maple Bear Global Schools
www.maplebear.ca

Author of: *Raising Global Nomads: Parenting Abroad in an On-Demand World, 2006*

A Moveable Marriage: Relocate Your Relationship Without Breaking It, 2003

Homeward Bound: A Spouse's Guide to Repatriation, 2000

A Broad Abroad: The Expat Wife's Guide to Successful Living Abroad, 1993

Culture Shock! Living and Working Abroad: A Parent's Guide, 1993

INTRODUCTION

My 'aha' moment happened on a trip back to my home country of Pakistan. Like many expats living abroad, trips back 'home' had become an uncomfortable experience for me. Instead of warmth and familiarity, I felt displacement and loss. I hated feeling like I didn't belong to the place where I had once fit in so well. After my early childhood as an expat kid in Bahrain and the United States, my family had repatriated, and I had grown up in Karachi, Pakistan. Its sights and sounds had fed my soul, I had grown up eating its delicious mangoes and walking the chaotic streets full of noisy *rickshaws*, wearing colorful *shalwar kameezes*, and loving the unhurried pace and vibrancy of life there.

I had last lived in Karachi when I was a 19-year-old teenager. Now, 16 years later, I found myself sitting in my parents' living room as a 35-year-old mother of two. The marble floor remained untouched, but the furniture had completely changed over the years, making the space feel like an odd mixture of past and present. What made me feel at home though were the old family photos on the TV stand, taken in Central Park, Niagara Falls and in Disneyland.

"Let's take you shopping," Mummy declared clapping her hands together. Salma, my older sister, moved closer to me and handed me a cup of chai.

"It will be just like old times, except now we mostly shop at Dolmen Mall!" Salma added.

"But I don't want to go to a shopping mall and buy readymade clothes. Can't we go to one of the bazaars and buy fabric the way we used to and design our own clothes with the help of the tailor? Mummy, do you still have that tailor in Gizri we used to love?"

Mummy laughed and said, "I think the last time I got anything stitched was at your wedding, Mariam! Now it's all about convenience, most people just go buy clothes that are already stitched. Life in Pakistan has gotten hectic. Who has time to design clothes themselves now?"

I sipped my chai quietly. Yet another thing that had changed since I had left. I realized how different our perspectives had become. What in my mind was a special and unique aspect of living here, was for my family a hassle they were eager to move beyond. Tiny exchanges like these cemented my feelings of no longer belonging to my hometown. My family joked I had become more Pakistani while living abroad and I wondered for the first time if there was any truth to this. My marriage to Martino, my half German/half Italian husband, and our two kids Mina and Mikail, meant that I was always consciously fighting to preserve the Pakistani identity in our multicultural family. One way in which I was doing this was trying to speak with my kids in Urdu, our native tongue. But each time we visited Pakistan, my parents, my sister and my extended family all continued to speak mostly English to them and the lack of support and understanding often left me weary and demotivated.

As I sat there thinking about past shopping trips, I thought back to how much fun it used to be to buy our own fabric.

The beauty of looking at a piece of cloth and envisioning what it could become.

The thrill of deciding whether to buy chiffon or silk and which embellishments and buttons would look best.

The excitement of designing something unique.

The control in having your say on the material and how to stitch it.

The anticipation of picking up your final design from the tailor.

The pure joy in wearing something that expressed who you are.

In none of the countries that I had lived in after Pakistan, was designing your own clothes possible. In Houston I shopped at the Galleria Mall in Midtown, and in Brighton I shopped at quirky boutiques in The Lanes. In Berlin shopping on the Ku'damm had been my routine, while in Copenhagen, there was an H&M at every corner down Strøget. In Singapore my expat life revolved around Orchard Road and its many glitzy malls. I was now living in Dubai and could shop at Harvey Nichols or Dolce Gabbana but somehow shopping in Karachi was still my favorite because it was the only place where I could create something unique that showed who I was and then wear it proudly. At least, that's how I *thought* it was.

And that's when it hit me. I no longer designed my own clothes. In fact, I had not done so for well over a decade. However, thanks to a globally mobile life, I was still busy designing my life story. Each country I moved to was stitched onto my story in some shape or form. Each of the languages I picked up along the way helped me sew my story together and each culture I was exposed to shaped my overall design.

After all these moves, what story was I stitching together?

This messy, multicultural and multilingual life on the move, which sometimes didn't make sense and most days left me feeling overwhelmed and reeling outside of my comfort zone was not disjointed pieces of a fabric. It was not easy to turn the jumble of scraps that each represented a piece of me and my family into a beautiful, wearable garment I could be proud of. It may not have been easy, but it *was* possible. All the different cultures, races, religions, languages, identities, homes, belonging and experiences were being stitched onto my design – every day, with every move, with every experience – without me being consciously aware of it. *Now,* I wondered, *could I help to make sense first of my own messy mobile life and add some cohesion to it and then could I maybe help others to do the same?*

INTRODUCTION TO A MOLA

I started looking for a metaphor to make sense of this messy, mobile life that was slowly forming a unique design. When I met my writing mentor Jo Parfitt in Dubai in November 2017, we sat down to brainstorm my ideas. She listened to me talk for two hours as I threw in a lot of words starting with 'M': "multicultural", "multilingual", "multi-mobile", "moving" and "messy" and then asked me if I knew another word that started with an 'M':

"Have you heard of a mola?"

I hadn't. But as soon as Jo started explaining what a mola was, I felt myself getting incredibly excited.

A mola is a South American piece of cloth, made and worn by the Guna, the indigenous people who live in Panama and Colombia today. In the Guna's native language, *mola* means 'shirt' or 'clothing.'

Molas are handmade using a reverse appliqué technique. Several layers (usually two to seven) of brightly-colored cloth (usually cotton) are sewn together; the design is then formed by cutting away parts of each layer. The edges of the layers are then turned under and sewn down by a process known as appliqué. Often, the stitches are nearly invisible. This is achieved by using a thread the same color as the layer being sewn, using very small blind stitches. The best molas have extremely fine stitching, made using tiny needles.

A mola is a unique piece of clothing. It represents who you are and allows you to 'show your lining' to the world. Sometimes, it is painful to show certain parts of your story; some layers hide beneath others and resurface when you least expect it. Some cuts are difficult, and it hurts. Others are easier and seamlessly incorporate into your overall design.

A mola is your life by design. It is complex and multi-layered, just like living a life on the move.

Figure 1: A typical mola pattern made by the Guna people in Panama.

For the next 12 months, I operated in a parallel universe consisting purely of molas. At night I dreamt of molas and during the day it was all I researched and could think of. My research led me to Norma McCaig, the founder of Global Nomads International and one of the early pioneers who had compared living a globally mobile life to designing a mola. As a Third Culture Kid herself, she had encouraged Third Culture Kids to embrace their life story, their experiences, identities and emotions through the mola concept and to wear theirs proudly in front of the world, as a way to embrace their uniqueness. In her foreword in the first edition of *The Third Culture Kid Experience: Growing Up Among Worlds* by Ruth E. Van Reken and David C. Pollock published in 1999, Norma wrote:

"The symbolism inherent in the construction of a mola, speaks to who I am as a global nomad. Each mola has the stamp of the creator's individuality but is borne of a distinct cultural heritage. So it is with our lives as global nomads, as TCKs."

I was inspired to take the concept of a mola and develop it further; to give it a whole framework to explain a life on the move that extended beyond TCKs as well. I also wanted to use the mola not just as a metaphor but as a toolbox, to help globally mobile families see the life they were creating by design.

And that's how the idea and inspiration behind this book came about: how can globally mobile families go from a mess to a mola?

But first...

WHY DO OUR GLOBAL LIVES GET MESSY?

Is it any wonder that when you leave behind everything you have known, your life will feel like a mess on most days? I realized that most books either dealt with the mobility experienced as a child and advised parents how to raise a Third Culture Kid or dealt with mobility as adults, advising how to plan for an international move. Or there were books that were still stuck in dealing with the traditional model of expatriation of two parents from the same country, followed by a repatriation to the same country. Where was all the real, honest-to-goodness advice that dealt with just how messy your life could become, with no easy answers? Where were the books on the new generation we were raising with multiple homes, multiple languages and multiple identities? I wanted a book on complex topics that are often dealt with separately – such as multicultural, multi-ethnic, multi-faith, multilingual, multi-moving families. I wanted to deal with them in one place.

I also wanted to give you, my reader, permission to take off those rose-tinted glasses and acknowledge that a mobile life is a messy life. You may be married to someone from a different culture, you are constantly exposed to new cultures, you are learning new languages and making new friends and just when you've figured out how your new washing machine works and how to help your kid do their homework in Mandarin, it's time to move on again, or move back 'home' and start all over again.

I wanted a book that dealt with *all* the messy factors in living this global life, not just one or two. When I could not find it, I decided to write it myself. I wanted this book to be a daring first attempt at embracing the messiness and diversity in our international lives. I wanted to empower you to feel you can live and celebrate this messy mobile life too.

In each of the chapters of this book, I share a story from my own global life in the hope that it will resonate with you. Yet I recognized that my stories alone would not be enough to inspire and inform you on your own journey. Who am I to think I know it all, right? To add some substance to my theories I decided to do two things. First, I would call upon the experts – the interculturalists, the transition coaches, the language experts, the mobility professionals, to get their opinions on the issues raised. Secondly, I would conduct '*The Mobile Family Survey*' in 2018 to research and understand which challenges global families were facing and which joys and benefits they enjoyed. I then sat down to chart the messy threads one by one. Armed with my own stories, the results of the survey and a group of nine experts, I set to work to debunk the myths and provide tips, strategies and advice to help us all – my own family included – to make sense of our marvelous yet messy mobile lives.

To make this book truly add value for my reader, I also decided to go a step further. I decided to use the mola not just as a concept, but also as a tool that would help you and your family to navigate your own messy mobile lives. Thus, in this book, I equip you with your own MOLA toolbox so you can start to untangle the messy threads, just like I did for my family.

WHO THIS BOOK IS FOR AND WHY IT WILL MAKE A DIFFERENCE

This is a guidebook aimed at two audiences. Its primary audience is globally mobile families living around the world. Its secondary audience is those who support globally mobile families in their lives overseas through their work. By explaining the inner workings of the globally mobile family, this book is a powerful tool for international companies, HR departments, global mobility specialists, international and bilingual schools and relocation agencies to understand the challenges they face and provide realistic support, assistance and understanding.

This book doesn't just explain how a globally mobile family works, but it also helps key stakeholders such as HR professionals and international schools to build a real appreciation of the families they serve. For example, schools can use it as a built-in curricular tool or as part of an introductory questionnaire for new families. HR departments and global mobility specialists can use the book to share with their employees ahead of their next international move to ensure they have done their homework and have a framework and understanding of how to create their own mobile life by design.

It does not matter whether you call yourself a Third Culture Kid (TCK), a Cross-Cultural Kid (CCK), an Adult TCK (ATCK), a Third Culture Adult (TCA), an expatriate, an immigrant, a migrant worker, a diplomat, a missionary, an international or a global nomad. If you have moved from one country to another regardless of the reason and circumstances, you are creating your own mola and your own MOLA Family, so this book is for you. This is a unique book in that it seeks to explain a mobile life not from an individual perspective, but from a family perspective. The family remains at the core of the book and its ideas.

This book will help you and your family make sense of your messy mobile life and figure out how to thrive when handling the messy factors you will encounter. Through the help of advice from experts, you will be able to stitch together the different components of your international life to see which patterns are emerging. Through introducing the MOLA as not just a concept but also a tool will help you to embrace your life story and thrive in who you are becoming. It is a way for you to tell your life story.

It gives you permission to embrace who you are and wear it on your sleeve for the whole world to see. It is also malleable and responsive – a mola can be changed, updated, drawn upon, or unsewn.

In sharing the MOLA with you, I wanted to share one of the best tools to navigate your messy, mobile life. I hope it will help you and your family, as much as it has helped me and my family.

Mariam Navaid Ottimofiore,
Accra, Ghana, 2019

www.andthenwemovedto.com

f /andthenwemovedto

@andthenwemoved2

@andthenwemovedto

in linkedin.com/in/mariamottimofiore

WHAT THIS BOOK WILL DO FOR YOUR FAMILY

. . . .

I wrote *This Messy Mobile Life* to help globally mobile families; multicultural, multilingual and multi-mobile families understand who they are, what they are creating and how to benefit from owning and sharing their life story. Each of the following chapters is made up of practical tips, advice and strategies on various aspects of your messy mobile life and goes on to include an exercise for you to complete with your family. In addition, each chapter includes conversation starters for you to explore together.

In short, this book will help your family in three important ways: it will encourage you to make sense of your globally mobile life, it will equip you with the MOLA toolbox on how to go from a mess to a mola and it will inspire you to claim your story and share it with others to reap the benefits of your journey.

IT WILL ENCOURAGE YOU TO MAKE SENSE OF YOUR GLOBALLY MOBILE LIFE

When you live a life on the move, you are constantly adding new experiences, countries, cultures, languages, identities and so much more to your life story. Each move involves gains and losses, but often you forget to reflect on the end result. What are all these global experiences leading to? Who are you becoming? How is your family culture changing? What have you found yourself insisting upon? What challenges have shaped you and which opportunities have you enjoyed the most?

This Messy Mobile Life will help you to make sense of your globally mobile life by 'joining the dots' between its component parts. It will show you how factors like your cultures, languages and mobility are contributing to your overall life story and how to deal with the challenges they throw in your way. It will help you to see what issues stand out for your family and how to address them. It will also show you how to enjoy the benefits of your global life and give you important rules on dealing with each 'messy' thread.

... EQUIP YOU WITH THE MOLA TOOLBOX HELPING YOU TO GO FROM MESS TO MOLA

This book is designed to give you and your family a toolbox for navigating through your global lives. My MOLA toolbox consists of four specific components you need to go from a mess to a MOLA Family. Thus, in my MOLA framework, a MOLA is an acronym, and I explain what the M, O, L and A stand for in each chapter.

When you are creating your MOLA Family, it helps to think of the M, O and the L as 'the what' and the A as 'the how.' Together, they form your MOLA toolbox and show you how to create your MOLA and use it to steer your way successfully through your global life.

... INSPIRE YOU TO OWN YOUR STORY

Last but not least, this book will help you and inspire you to own your family life story and to share it proudly with the world. Towards the end of the book, I teach you how to 'show' your mola to those who matter; from international schools, to your multinational corporations and organizations, to relocation agencies, to your extended families, to other MOLA Families and to people in your home country and host country.

I chose the concept of a mola for this book because in South America a mola is a shirt that you wear to show the world who you are. It is something you put on every day, and wear proudly, as it represents your unique heritage and story. I want this book to inspire you and your family to proudly wear your mola, your life story for all the world to see.

A mola is not meant to be hidden in a corner somewhere in your wardrobe where it gathers dust. If you hide it, you negate all the wonderful experiences that have given you your unique design. You are denying part of who you are. But if you show your mola, you display its richness and have the power to understand your place in the world.

HOW TO USE THIS BOOK

This book is a blend of rich insights into messy global lives, and at the same time a workbook and toolbox designed to help you think and look at your mobile life in a creative way. I advise that the first time you read it should be from cover to cover, to understand the full mola concept and the MOLA framework. But you may find that certain chapters relate to your family more, and I encourage you to bookmark them and return to them again.

As I introduce concepts, I support them with examples of families and situations, and provide expert insights to enable you to find parallels with your own situation. You may also find that the more familiar you become with the tools, the more you can decode/decipher your own situation and that of those around you.

Keep a pencil handy to jot down notes and do your exercises at the end of each chapter. I also encourage you to keep a MOLA notebook, to write down ideas and themes that pop into your mind as you read along. You can of course enjoy doing this with your children too.

You can engage in the conversation starters at the dining table as a family activity that can help you explore several themes together. I include conversation starters in each chapter because I find that having small, everyday conversations helps you process your messy mobile life as it continues to swirl around you. Often, there are certain crunch times when the messiness in our lives is really revealed – for example when visitors come and pass judgment, when certain holidays carry certain expectations, or when different priorities around family commitments means one partner feels more strongly about getting on a plane than another. It's at these crunch times, however, that there is even less time than normal to address the issues! By offering families a conversation starter, I hope you can have these conversations at times that are not frantic and pave the way for better understanding when things do get frantic.

Throughout the book, I use mola/MOLA a lot. Just remember:

Mola = the shirt

MOLA = your toolbox as an acronym and a MOLA Family.

For example: "a MOLA Family makes its mola."

I hope you enjoy reading this book! If you have any questions or comments as you create your MOLA, feel free to email me at mariamottimofiore@gmail.com or head to my website www.andthenwemovedto.com for many more things MOLA.

CHAPTER ONE

FROM MESS TO MOLA!

. . . .

"The magic lies in the mess."
Brené Brown

MY MESSY INTERNATIONAL LIFE

DUBAI, UNITED ARAB EMIRATES, 2017:

I see him watching us carefully. Not in a creepy way, but rather in a half fascinated, half curious, way. I watch him glance first at my husband and then at our kids, who are splashing around in the sprawling resort pool. Then a quick glance back at me when I turn to say something to our children. A look of confusion crosses his face, then excitement, before he hesitates to listen to our conversation more carefully and quietly observes the four of us interacting in three languages. He notes the colors of our skin, the accent on our tongues, the tan lines on some of us and our various levels of comfort in the water. Finally putting the pieces of the jigsaw together he turns to his wife, a few meters away from him in the water, and says in German:

1

"Well, the father is definitely speaking German, even though he looks more Mediterranean – probably some Spanish or Italian influence there. The wife looks Persian, but I think she's speaking an Indian language with the children. I think they must live here in Dubai, they seem more used to the heat than us!"

It's always interesting to hear how a perfect stranger describes you and your family. All it has taken him are a few minutes of observation to understand we are a multicultural and multilingual family, living in another country.

He doesn't realize that I am close enough to hear him and that I understand what he is saying. I turn to him with a smile and say in German:

"Those are some great observations indeed! You are quite close on most of them!"

His shock is apparent and embarrassment soon follows. I laugh his concerns away and instead take a closer look at him. Kind smile, gray hair, severely sunburnt – he seems to be around 60, probably enjoying a sunny holiday in the UAE with his wife and eager to do a spot of people-watching.

His next question though is more an observation than a question as he says:

"You are a beautiful family, but it must be complicated sometimes, no?"

My husband and I share a knowing glance and a smile.

'Complicated' does not begin to describe our fusion family. Our international lives are downright messy. Our family is like a rich, buttery marble cake, with chocolate swirls mixed in with the vanilla. A cake achieved by blending light and dark batters, which gives it a piebald appearance. Just as you can never predict how many, or how big

the streaks and swirls will turn out while baking your marble cake, we could never predict how our diverse cultural backgrounds would mesh together to form our own unique family blend.

UNTANGLING OUR INTERNATIONAL MESS

When people ask us where we are from, it is hard to know where to start. Do we explain where each of us was born, or the countries in which we have grown up, or the country in which we currently live? As a family, we have multiple identities that often jostle for attention. The four of us do not share the same birth country, the same first language, the same childhood memories nor the same view of the world. We are one family, yet all of us are different.

EXPAT CHILD TO EXPAT ADULT – MY JOURNEY

I was born in the bustling mega-metropolis of Karachi, Pakistan, a city by the Arabian Sea. At the time of my birth in 1982, my Pakistani parents were living as expatriates in the tiny Middle Eastern Kingdom of Bahrain. My mother decided to give birth to me in Pakistan, partly to be near family and partly to ensure that I could get a passport upon birth. Bahrain, like most countries in the Gulf, does not issue citizenship based on birth and back then, it was rather difficult to get a Pakistani passport if you were not born there. Worried that their newborn daughter would be stateless, my parents agreed to go back to Karachi to await my arrival. Unknown to me, my path in life was already set: an expat from birth and a scattering of homes around the world.

'Complicated' does not begin to describe our fusion family. Our international lives are downright messy. Our family is like a rich, buttery marble cake, with chocolate swirls mixed in with the vanilla. A cake achieved by blending light and dark batters, which gives it a piebald appearance. Just as you can never predict how many, or how big the streaks and swirls will turn out while baking your marble cake, we could never predict how our diverse cultural backgrounds would mesh together to form our own unique family blend.

When I was not even two years old, my father, a banker, received his next posting to New York City, which became our home until the end of the 80s. There, my parents focused on raising my sister and me as Pakistani Muslims living in the United States. We spoke Urdu at home and English outside in nursery and school (we loosely followed the language framework of Minority Language at Home, Majority Language Outside). I grew up this way, as a Third Culture Kid (TCK) and bilingual from birth. I was used to switching my accents and my words and figured out with whom to speak which language. When we moved back to Pakistan just in time for me to begin my formal schooling, I had a tough time adjusting to the heat but had no issues with the spoken languages. In addition to English, I learned how to write in Urdu, speak Sindhi (the local provincial language), read poetry in Persian and recite the Quran in Arabic.

After a decade of expat life, my parents were happy to be home. Pakistan soon became all I ever knew. The sound of the *muezzin* singing the call to prayer, the hot, humid, dusty summers with never-ending power shortages, and my big extended family who all lived on one street provided me with a powerful sense of Pakistani identity, comfort and security. Life ambled on predictably but the restlessness in my soul from my childhood never quite went away.

At the age of 19, I decided to leave home and go on a solo adventure. With a one-way ticket in my hand, I arrived at Boston's Logan Airport, just shortly after 9/11, to attend Mount Holyoke College in South Hadley, Massachusetts. The America of my childhood was changing fast and, as an adult, it felt like just any other foreign country. After only two years in the States, I decided to do my Junior Year Abroad – in England. Something about being at the Brighton pier made me feel at home. I realize I always feel at home in cities by the sea; it is the stamp my Karachi upbringing has left on my soul. England was the place where love arrived unexpectedly in the shape of a six-foot-tall, half-German/half-Italian boy.

A CROSS-CULTURAL KID – THE JOURNEY OF MY HUSBAND, MARTINO

It was definitely not love at first sight. Or second. Or even third. Instead, as I took my seat in the classroom for an orientation meeting for new international students, in the ivy-covered building on a beautiful English campus in Sussex, I gave him a look of annoyance. There he was – my future husband – sitting next to two other Italian students and speaking (and gesturing) very loudly in Italian.

Loud, obnoxious and full of himself were my first impressions as I observed him from a distance. His brown hair was long and wavy, baggy jeans hanging fashionably low, and he switched effortlessly between English and Italian as he chatted to those around him.

When the Dean of International Students asked us to introduce ourselves and mingle, he came over directly to me and said, "Hi, my name is Martino. I'm Italian."

With a name like that, I believed him.

It was only later when I got to know him properly, that I found out he is only half-Italian. He is also half-German and he was born in Germany, raised in Germany and lived in Germany too. But from the time he was labeled as an Italian on the school playground, to his annual visits to his father's hometown in Sicily, he has strongly identified as an Italian. Years later, when I teased him about not telling me the whole truth, he replied with a grin, "When I meet a girl I like, I'm always an Italian."

A product of a cross-cultural marriage, Martino grew up in two cultures from the time of his birth in 1980 in Wolfsburg, Germany. His Italian father had come from Sicily to Germany as a *Gastarbeiter* (guest worker) in the mid-60s, to look for work. Not only did he find work, but he also met a German girl and decided to settle down in Germany. Together they raised their only son as both German and Italian (with a touch of Sicilian!). It was a predominantly Protestant Christian upbringing, since my father-in-law described himself as only a 'lukewarm Catholic.'

As a true Cross-Cultural Kid (CCK), Martino grew up bilingually from birth as well: his family practiced the popular 'One Person, One Language' (OPOL) framework to teach him both German and Italian. In addition, Martino learned English, Spanish and French through school and became equally proficient in these five languages. A high school year abroad in Nebraska, Omaha, in the United States, cemented his English, while repeated work and internships in Spain and Argentina cemented his ability to do business in Spanish. Working abroad had always interested him and he spent his summer months interning in South Africa one year, then in Canada the next.

"Mr. Darcy improves upon acquaintance," explains Elizabeth Bennet in Jane Austen's *Pride and Prejudice*. Similarly, once I became friends with Martino and got to know him better, I realized he was a funny, caring, ambitious, loyal and rather handsome man (did I not mention he was half-Italian?). His personality was a perfect mix of the two cultures he had grown up in since birth. When it came to his studies or his work, he was organized, efficient and punctual, but when it came to relationships, family and food he was spontaneous, warm and adventurous. I felt so comfortable around him, as if I had known him all my life but, how could I have? We had grown up in opposite corners of the world.

He played football, and I was a cricket fanatic.

He grew up on pasta and lasagnas, while I grew up on spicy *biryanis*.

His cultural references were post-Berlin Wall and the evolution of the *mafia* in Sicily, and mine were pre-nuclear Pakistan and post-9/11 America.

We were as different as East from West yet shared the same interests: a love for travel, cultures, languages, politics and the desire to experience the world for ourselves.

In all likelihood, we would have parted at the end of our study year abroad in England as good friends who perhaps kept in touch over Facebook or email.

Instead, we fell recklessly in love.

OUR MULTICULTURAL MARRIAGE

When it came time to plan our wedding, I was living and working in Houston, Texas, while my parents were in Karachi, Pakistan. Martino was living in Buenos Aires, Argentina, where he was working at a law firm, while his parents were living in Wolfsburg, Germany. Through this complicated four-way communication over different time zones, we coordinated each aspect of our upcoming wedding. My lovely older sister Salma took on the role of being the planner and helped us set up a wedding website to share and exchange ideas from both sides.

Our multicultural wedding took place in two countries and five languages and was attended by people of over 20 different nationalities. The invitation to our wedding ceremonies in Germany was printed in German, Italian and English while the invitation to our wedding in Pakistan was printed in Urdu, Arabic and English. Speeches made to toast us had to be translated twice or even three times sometimes. When making a seating plan, our only criterion was to place guests at the same table if they spoke at least one language in common!

Our first wedding took place in Martino's hometown in Germany, where guests had to constantly change outfits to attend first our civil ceremony at a 16th-century medieval German castle, then to cover their heads in a mosque to participate in our Islamic marriage ceremony, before sitting down for an eight-course Italian meal for our wedding reception at an Italian restaurant.

Figure 2: Image of our wedding invitation in German, Italian and English.

A few months later, we had a traditional wedding ceremony in Pakistan, complete with a *mehnd*i night of music, songs and dancing and a *rukhsati* which is the wedding reception thrown by the bride's parents. I wanted to stick to our family tradition of being married at my grandparents' house next door to ours, where many of my generation were married in the bougainvillea-laced gardens under the twinkling lights. The Germans and Italians who had flown into Karachi for the wedding wore their first *shalwar kameezes* and *saris* (traditional Pakistani attire). Cultural confusions were many; unfamiliar norms regarding weddings were explained and guests needed to be de-briefed repeatedly. Unsurprisingly, attendance at both the weddings was sky high due to the interest our cross-cultural union had sparked. Despite the differences, our ceremony was conducted in the spirit of love, tolerance and harmony. Our love was celebrated with traditional Pakistani music in the form of *qawwali* (Sufi inspired melodies) and with love songs sung in traditional Sicilian fashion performed live by a Sicilian band.

9

Just to be sure, we had been married in every possible way – we had sawed through German wood together while our families cheered us on, as per a German wedding ritual which tries to prepare the husband and wife to work together as a team. We had kissed each time our Italian family had shouted *"Bacio! Bacio!"* And we had sat next to each other, as relatives from each side stuffed Pakistani *gulab jamuns* (deep-fried balls made of butter, flour and milk, soaked in rose-water scented sugar syrup) in our mouths, placed henna on the palm of my hands to symbolize fertility, and had even stolen one of Martino's shoes in exchange for money!

When Martino finally paid up (after endless negotiations and bargaining with my cousins in several different currencies), he was allowed to leave with me as his wife and take me to the 5-star hotel booked for our wedding night. With the Quran held high over my head as a symbol of protection, my parents, sister, cousins, extended family and grandparents walked me out to my new life. It was an emotional moment – my grandmother couldn't hold back her tears, and neither could I. I don't want to even imagine how my mother felt.

Martino helped me maneuver my long red, wedding *gharara, dupatta* and heavy gold jewelry to climb inside our getaway car, which had been decorated in red roses and yellow marigolds in typical Pakistani fashion to signify our newlywed status. In a few weeks we would honeymoon in the Caribbean (a wedding present from my in-laws) but for the next week, we stayed in Pakistan to give my extended family the chance to throw lavish lunches and dinners in honor of our wedding.

I remember looking at Martino that night in Karachi, thinking what an exercise in international relations and global logistics we had just attempted. We held hands tightly in the car, almost too afraid to look at each other and to let it sink in that we had finally made our union possible. The promise we had made to be with each other, standing on the shores of the Brighton Beach in England had seemed so impossible and yet here we were. Our Pakistani hotel room was booked under my name, "Mrs. Mariam" – my uncle who had arranged the booking for us told me they charged foreigners more for a hotel room, so the room was under my name and not Martino's! We laughed and joked and learned early on how to use our various names to our advantage depending on which country we were in. Little did I know that this cultural tap dance was just the tip of the iceberg.

Our adventures were just getting started.

In the twelve years since, we have spent our married life living in Germany, Denmark, Singapore, the United Arab Emirates and Ghana. Along the way, we have had two children, born in two different countries, more than 3,000 miles apart. We have spent the past six years raising our children outside all three of their passport countries – Germany, Pakistan and Italy. Home for them is Singapore and Dubai, and currently Accra. At the time of writing this chapter we were still living in Dubai, although by the time I had finished writing the book, we had made a move to Accra, Ghana.

HELPING YOU UNTANGLE THE MESS

The first step towards understanding a multicultural, multilingual and multi-mobile family involves untangling the *mess*. To take each separate thread and study it in isolation before understanding how it contributes to your final design. So how can I help you untangle the mess that is your international family? You may feel that you have been largely left to your own devices and have had to figure this all out by yourself. You have resigned yourself to using trial and error and seeing what works for your family and what doesn't. Sometimes it feels like you are not in control. This approach will help you take back the control as we tackle each messy thread one by one.

PRIDE AND APPRECIATION OF ONE'S OWN HERITAGE

"Children raised from the early years with a pride and appreciation of their total heritage have the best chance of developing into secure adults," explains Dr. Francis Wardle, an expert in multicultural studies, who has published two books on multiracial children alongside several journal articles on multicultural families in the United States.

For many mobile families, addressing this is the first step in understanding your family's story. It is important to expose your children to their diverse heritage. To teach them about their culture, race and background and give them a context to place themselves and their lives in. Being culturally aware of your surroundings means first being aware of your own family history and heritage.

TAKING ACTION – PURPOSEFULLY BLENDING CULTURES

"Ongoing, consistent, sustainable cultural awareness is not natural inside the home or out. So, living globally as a multicultural family can be double jeopardy. It's far too easy to take the richness of diversity that comes with a global life for granted," explains Jerry Jones, an American cross-cultural trainer, author of the book *99 Questions For Global Families* and writer at The Culture Blend.

Blending cultures is the next step in making sense of your messy global lives. As Jerry explains, this often means families have to be intentional and purposeful about what they are creating:

"The key is to do what is not natural and to do it with great intentionality. It's perfectly natural to let the beauty of the cultures represented in your home and your community drift toward the back of your consciousness. Intentionality then, is making a conscious decision and a purposeful effort to bring them back to the front. Blending cultures in a multicultural, global family must be purposeful, premeditated, proactive and tremendously intentional."

"Blending cultures in a multicultural, global family must be purposeful, premeditated, proactive and tremendously intentional."

— Jerry Jones.

LANGUAGE AND MULTILITERACY

The next messy thread is language and a family goal of multiliteracy for their children. When it comes to learning, supporting and sustaining different languages in multilingual families, intentionality and preparation are key factors too.

"We speak many languages in our family and community. Maintaining them all and supporting our children's multiliteracy is a challenge especially when these languages are not all supported by school," explains multilingual language consultant and coach Dr. Ute Limacher-Riebold from Ute's International Lounge, who helps to coach multilingual parents around the world.

THE IMPACT OF MOBILITY ON YOUR PARENTING

How do parents deal with the challenges of parenting in different countries and cultures and how does mobility affect the way you parent? Dealing with the complexities of raising children in a culture different than your own poses its share of unique challenges notes Valérie Besanceney, author of the children's book *B at Home: Emma Moves again*, Adult TCK and International School Teacher.

"Once you raise your child in a different culture than your own, you will have to accept that your child will probably never identify with your culture in the same way you do. Although this may feel like a threat to your own 'family culture', it is actually a wonderful opportunity to embrace the cultures that touch your life, to consciously celebrate your own culture(s), and provide your child with a strong sense of roots in both. The earlier your children feel that you wholeheartedly acknowledge the difference in your and their cultural experiences, the more you will help your children value the uniqueness of their experiences and help them develop a grounded sense of identity," says Valérie.

MY FAMILY'S OWN EXPERIENCE

When I started this process with regards to my own family, I had no blueprint. I knew no experts on blending cultures, no family language coaches and no other families struggling with the same mobility issues that I was. There was no framework to refer to, no written experiences to learn from and no other books written that combined multiculturalism, multilingualism and mobility in international families. Often books dealt with each of these topics separately, but never as a whole. I grew increasingly frustrated researching books that seemed to be missing complex narratives and dealt only with bilingualism or dealt only with a cross-cultural marriage or addressed only the challenges of living abroad. I wanted to know what happens when you combine cultures, languages and mobility in one family.

Where were the books on what happens *after* you raise your bilingual kid and he meets and marries another bilingual speaker? What happens *after* your Adult Third Culture Kid meets and marries a Cross-Cultural Kid and tries to blend their lives together? What happens when between you and your partner, you have no clear home base *because* of the globally mobile lifestyle you have grown up living?

Where were the books on what happens after you raise your bilingual kid and he meets and marries another bilingual speaker? What happens after your Third Culture Kid meets and marries a Cross-Cultural Kid and tries to blend their lives together? What happens when between you and your partner, you have no clear home base because of the globally mobile lifestyle you have grown up living?

Note: For a full explanation of terms like Third Culture Kid (TCK), Adult Third Culture Kid (ATCK) and Cross-Cultural Kid (CCK), see the Glossary.

INTRODUCING A "MOLA FAMILY"

Polish CCK and Egyptian ATCK in UAE

Julia is Polish and born in Poland but raised in Canada by her immigrant Polish parents. She met and married her husband in Canada, who is Egyptian and was born in Egypt but grew up in Kuwait and Canada. Soon after their marriage, they moved together to the United Arab Emirates, where their first daughter was born.

"Even though we are both Canadian, we don't think of it as home, or the places we were born in as home. We are looking for home I guess, hoping to find it in transit," explains Julia.

In this book, I call Julia's family a MOLA Family.

What is a MOLA Family? As I have already described in the *Introduction* a mola is a South American piece of cloth, made and worn by the Guna, the indigenous people who live in Panama and Colombia today. In the Guna's native language, *mola* means 'shirt' or 'clothing.'

Molas are handmade using a reverse appliqué technique. In her foreword in the first edition of *The Third Culture Kid Experience: Growing Up Among Worlds* by Ruth E. Van Reken and David C. Pollock published in 1999, Norma McCaig explains best how a mola is made:

"Pieces of brightly-colored fabrics, as many as five to eight, are layered upon one another and attached temporarily at each corner. The seamstress cuts down to different layers, folds the edges under in the desired shape to reveal the color beneath and stitches the folds in place. As she continues to cut, fold and stitch, a multi-hued pattern slowly emerges, finally coming together in a richly vibrant image of a fish or a lobster for instance. The end result is a piece that has a solid hue on one side and emerges brilliantly into full color on the other side."

A MOLA Family is thus a family that stitches together its own mola using its multicultural heritage as the fabric of its shirt, its multilingual make-up as the thread to sew the shirt together and its multi-mobile experiences to produce the different layers and ultimately provide the design of its mola.

Just like a mola, a MOLA Family is a complex design. Its multicultural heritage includes all the different cultures, races, ethnicities, religions and nationalities present in that family. Its multilingual composition and all the languages that the family members speak are the threads that bind the family together and help them to communicate with one another. And its multi-mobile lifestyle means the family takes its international experiences, the different identities, homes and sense of belonging to give its mola a multitude of layers and a design. A MOLA Family is never final, it continually adds layers to its design. Sometimes, it also needs to cut through those layers, to reveal the richness that lies underneath.

Figure 3: Hand-stitched mola from Panama, depicting fish, stars and animals.

DIFFERENT CHARACTERISTICS AND TYPES OF MOLA FAMILIES

MOLA Families come in all shapes and sizes. You could be a MOLA Family if, like us, you and your partner come from different countries and cultures and raise your children around the world with several languages. I collected data from hundreds of international families through *The Mobile Family Survey* in 2018, through which participants shared their experiences from around the world. Here are some examples:

Same Passport but Adopted Children from a Different Country or Race

You could be a MOLA Family if you and your partner both come from the same country but have adopted a child (or children) from a different country, culture or race thus blending to create your multiracial and multicultural family.

Louisa and her husband are both Canadian citizens who have lived in Canada, the United States and Mexico.

"Our first three children are biological and are the same race as my husband and I. We then adopted our two youngest in Mexico. They are still quite young and are not fully impacted yet by the struggles of race personally, but it is something my husband and I and our older children are processing," explains Louisa.

Same Country but Different Cultural Backgrounds

You could be a MOLA Family if you and your partner come from the same country but from different cultural backgrounds.

Elaine and her husband are both British nationals, but her husband has Sri Lankan heritage, born to Sri Lankan parents in the UK and raised with Sri Lankan and British culture. Together they have raised their three mixed-race children in England, Dubai and Laos.

"Our children's skin tones have diluted from our first child being much darker than our third. I wouldn't say it's an issue, just something we are aware of as people often ask if all three children are ours, if we are out separately," mentions Elaine.

Same Country but Children Born and Raised in Different Countries

You could be a MOLA Family even if both parents come from the same country, share the same nationality and speak the same language, but your children are born in different countries, and new languages, cultures and identities are adopted by your family because of your globally mobile lifestyle.

Lucille and her husband are both South African, although Lucille also holds British and Dutch nationalities and grew up as a Third Culture Kid (TCK). Their three children, born in Turkey, South Africa and the Netherlands are growing up amidst a plethora of new cultures and languages.

"I am very confused as to where my home is, so I can identify this feeling in my kids. My kids were all born in different countries but identify South Africa as home, even though we do not have a home there and they lived there for only three years. My youngest son will probably not feel South African. We talk about this a lot with the kids. The question 'Where are you from?' has an inside and an outside answer. Outside being where you were born or passport country (or countries), and inside being where you feel your home country is," says Lucille.

There are thus varying degrees of complexities in a MOLA Family. Each mola is unique. Your mola might contain a simpler pattern if your family is multicultural but not mobile or it might have an incredibly intricate pattern if your family is multicultural, multilingual and multi-mobile like ours.

A MOLA FAMILY IS...

Here are some of the typical characteristics a MOLA Family may share:

- Between the parents and the children, the MOLA Family has more than one cultural influence either at home or outside or both.
- Members of a MOLA Family may come from different races, but not necessarily.
- Members of a MOLA Family may speak more than one language at home or outside the home to communicate with the local community. This could also be true if you speak more than one regional language or a different dialect at home.
- Members of a MOLA Family may be born in different countries and may not have the same passports.
- Members of a MOLA Family may not have one home country but several because the father might come from Country A, the mother from Country B, they might have met in Country C and then had their first child in Country D, their second in Country E and then raised them in Country F.

- MOLA Family members are used to eating different foods and cuisines at home due to the diverse cultural influences present in their lives.

- MOLA Families frequently feel more attachment to other MOLA Families who are functioning on multicultural, multilingual and/or globally mobile backgrounds, than to a family who might share one home country or one home language with them.

- A MOLA Family may not know how to answer the ubiquitous question, "Where are you from?" knowing that each member of their family might cite a different city or country.

- A MOLA Family may not know which country to repatriate to after living overseas.

- A MOLA Family may celebrate more than one religious holiday at home.

- A MOLA Family may be used to wearing different traditional dresses depending on which country they are in.

- A MOLA Family may identify with the labels 'Third Culture Kid/TCK', 'Third Culture Adult/TCA', 'Cross-Cultural Kid/CCK', 'Adult Third Culture Kid/ATCK', 'expat', 'immigrant', 'migrant', 'global nomad', 'global citizen', 'international', 'global nomad' but not have an overall term to describe their whole family. I think we need such a term and, in my book, I call them a 'MOLA Family.'

CHALLENGES AND OPPORTUNITIES OF A MOLA FAMILY

MOLA Families try to combine their diversity just like you might try to combine the ingredients before getting ready to bake that marble cake. But not only is the result unpredictable, the process also comes with its own share of challenges and opportunities. You don't know the size or quantity of your chocolate swirls, nor what final pattern your cake will have.

MOLA Families are also a bit like my favorite fruit: the pomegranate. Pomegranates may look a bit boring on the outside but are full of rich gems on the inside. Some MOLA Families face so many challenges that they become like a pomegranate and start hiding who they are in the outside world. This is a real shame because MOLA Families can truly only shine when they are not afraid to share their mola with the outside world. It is important to remember that for every challenge that a MOLA Family may face, there is also a unique opportunity that this lifestyle brings forth.

A MOLA FAMILY MAY FACE:

Challenges

- **Race:** Family members may not look like one another. The children in a MOLA Family may feel conflicted as to which race they belong to.
- **Religion:** Family members may have different religious upbringings and struggle to decide how to raise their children.
- **Language:** When both parents are bilingual or multilingual, it can be challenging deciding which language to speak to your children. Or when your partner does not understand your mother tongue, that could complicate your family's language dynamics.
- **Culture:** A MOLA Family must often reconcile different cultural expectations with regards to work, life, family and parenting.
- **Identity:** A MOLA Family may struggle to reconcile multiple identities of its family members. A MOLA Family may never have one complete family identity.
- **Belonging:** A MOLA Family may experience a split sense of belonging (parts that don't add up to a whole).

- **Sense of home:** Home might be different for every family member. Trips back to home countries may be challenging when, for example, only one person out of four feels at home there. Parents might feel homesick for their home country while their kids might feel homesick for their host country.

- **Family traditions:** Which traditions do you adopt and celebrate as a family? Which do you let go? A MOLA Family might struggle to achieve this balance given their different childhoods and family culture.

- **Travel:** International travel may prove complicated with different passports, different visas and vaccines required to go to the same destination.

- **Dealing with in-laws and extended families:** You may face cultural expectations that may not apply for your whole family. Traditions around birth, marriage or death may vary significantly.

- **Dealing with unresolved grief:** A MOLA Family who moves frequently may encounter different forms of loss and the children may struggle to reconcile the loss of friendships, pets, familiar places and homes.

- **Bullying, mental illness or delayed maturity:** The children in a MOLA Family may face some of these challenges because they look, sound or are perceived as different by their peers in school.

- **Friendships:** A MOLA Family may struggle to maintain friendships over different continents and struggle without having a support network.

- **Dealing with immigration laws:** A MOLA Family may find they either do not have the opportunity to become citizens of their host country or they may face many obstacles and challenges in their path to obtaining citizenship.

- **Community:** A MOLA Family may struggle to develop a sense of depth of community because of its mobile lifestyle.

- **Split family:** A MOLA Family may find themselves struggling with a split family if the husband must go to work in a foreign country, while the wife and children stay back in their home country.
- **Retirement**: Many MOLA Families do not know or cannot agree on where to retire, or how to plan for retirement when their lives have been spread over many different countries.
- **Integration:** A MOLA Family may struggle to integrate into their host country, particularly when faced with a homogenous culture.

Opportunities

- **Diversity:** A MOLA Family can experience diversity from birth, inside the home and outside the home.
- **A global outlook:** A MOLA Family grows up with a global outlook. The family members don't live their lives within walls and borders.
- **Ability to access many cultures:** A MOLA Family can simultaneously access many cultures and understand global perspectives from varying viewpoints.
- **Communication and language advantages:** Being multilingual gives a MOLA Family a communication edge and they can use their multiple languages for various purposes such as increased competitiveness in the labor market.
- **Empathy:** Children in a MOLA Family grow up learning to practice empathy for others, given their constant exposure to new and different people.
- **Resilience:** Kids growing up in a MOLA Family learn to be resilient in the face of moving and new international experiences.
- **Adaptability:** Adapting to new surroundings is a key characteristic of MOLA Families.

- **Self-motivation and independence:** Children in a MOLA Family learn the key skills of self-motivation and independence through their globally mobile lifestyle.

- **To break barriers and boundaries:** MOLA Families learn how to break barriers and overstep boundaries. They try to find something in common with everybody and do not let differences in race, class or background hold them back.

- **Job opportunities:** A MOLA Family has access to increased job opportunities because of their multiple nationalities, languages, intercultural expertise and global experiences.

- **Linguistic empathy:** A MOLA Family realizes they cannot function without practicing linguistic empathy – tolerance and understanding of each other and the languages they speak.

- **International friendships:** A MOLA Family enjoys their international friendships with people from all over the world.

- **Tighter nuclear family:** A MOLA Family may find that living on the move provides freedom to choose their own family culture and helps to cement tighter bonds in their nuclear family.

- **Opportunity to help extended family in home country:** A MOLA Family may feel fortunate to help extended family in their home countries either financially or through providing them an incentive to travel and visit them abroad.

- **Safety:** A MOLA Family may enjoy increased safety overseas, if the parents hail from a developing or third world country.

THE FIVE RULES – TURN YOUR MESS INTO A MOLA!

1. UNDERSTAND THE CHALLENGES

The first rule towards turning your mess into a MOLA, is to understand the challenges. Combining diverse cultures, countries, nationalities, languages, races, homes and identities is not a process that comes easily and is not without its share of challenges. It is going to be messy. Use the conversation starters at the end of this chapter to identify and pinpoint your family challenges.

2. ACKNOWLEDGE THE DIFFERENCES

Do not gloss over your differences. Even tiny differences such as your definition of warm or chilly weather versus your partner's may differ greatly! Acknowledging your differences is the second rule towards creating your MOLA Family. A MOLA Family celebrates its differences and is conscious of them and the way they influence their family life. The best way to acknowledge your differences is to start talking about them candidly. For example you may turn to your partner and say: "I may be more hands-off when taking our children to the playground. In my culture, we teach kids the importance of independence at a young age. I am not ignoring our kids, I am giving them the freedom to play and learn." Enjoy sharing your own family stories with your parents and your children. Grandparents can be a fascinating source of insight for children and can help demonstrate how different things are today not only for your children but for you as a parent now.

3. ACCEPT YOUR LIFE WON'T BE THE SAME

If you grew up in a monocultural family, you need to accept that the family life you create will be different from the one you grew up in. If you have married someone from a different culture, your family life will need more negotiation, more compromise and more understanding of a different way of doing things. For example, it might take you and your partner longer to agree on what an acceptable bedtime may be for your children. If you have married someone from the same culture but lead a globally mobile lifestyle, then your family culture will differ starkly from your own upbringing. Your children may feel more comfortable eating with chopsticks than with forks and knives or singing 'happy birthday' to each other in Arabic rather than English.

4. LEARN THAT CULTURAL MISUNDERSTANDINGS WILL STILL HAPPEN

Even in a perfect MOLA Family, cultural misunderstandings will still happen. The more you understand the different cultures in your mola, the easier it will be to detect these misunderstandings and you'll be in a better position to deal with them. MOLA Families may never figure out all the issues of contention, but they can develop the right toolbox to deal with them, as identified in the chapters ahead.

5. COMMUNICATE TO ENSURE CULTURE IS NOT THE SCAPEGOAT

This can be tricky to avoid. It is easy to blame all differences on culture but making culture the scapegoat is never a good idea. In the end, you cannot simply blame culture for your fights and disagreements. It is important to communicate and take responsibility for your actions. A different culture should also never be the reason to tolerate verbal, emotional or physical abuse.

CHAPTER SUMMARY

1. Helping you to untangle your messy international lives is the first step. A mola, with its many layers, patterns, colors and designs, can help to make sense of a multicultural, multilingual and multi-mobile family life by showing how the messy details fit onto one shirt.

2. A MOLA Family can be multicultural, multilingual, multiracial, multi-mobile or any combination of factors. A MOLA Family can take on many different shapes and forms and come in all sizes.

3. Each MOLA Family faces certain challenges along the way. These could be cultural, linguistic, racial or due to mobility and transition.

4. Each MOLA Family also enjoys the various opportunities and advantages of living a globally mobile life such as access to many different cultures and languages, fostering resilience and adaptability in children and experiencing diversity.

5. To go from a mess to a MOLA, it is important to understand your unique challenges, acknowledge the differences in your family, accept your family life will be more complex than a family who is not globally mobile and understand how to handle the different cultures your family comes into contact with.

ACTIVITY: ARE YOU A MOLA FAMILY?

Which MOLA characteristics are present in your family? How 'messy' is your family? The exercise below is the first step in self-awareness and can be used to gauge your particular family situation. Using the columns below, you are going to make some lists:

List all the different cultures present in your family. List all the different languages you speak. List all the places you have lived in or have called home. List all the nationalities you hold. List the different races (if present) in your family. List how many children you have and add a row for more!

	Cultures	Races	Languages	Homes	Nationalities
Spouse 1					
Spouse 2					
Child 1					
Child 2					
Child 3					

MY MOLA FAMILY

Filling in the above chart, might make you realize that while you and your children may come from the same culture, perhaps your notion of home varies significantly, largely due to your globally mobile lifestyle.

Here is an image of what my chart looks like:

	Cultures	Races	Languages	Homes	Nationalities
Husband: Martino	German Italian	Caucasian/ White	German, Italian, French, Spanish, English and Urdu	Germany, Italy, USA, UK, Denmark, Singapore, UAE, Ghana, South Africa, Canada, Argentina	German Italian
Wife: Mariam	Pakistani American	South Asian/ Brown	Urdu, English, Hindi, German and Danish	Pakistan, Bahrain, USA, UK, Germany, Denmark, Singapore, UAE, Ghana	Pakistani Italian
Child 1: Mina	Singaporean, Emirati, German, Italian, Pakistani	Eurasian (mixed European and Asian descent)	Mandarin, Arabic, French, German, Italian, Urdu and English	Singapore, Dubai, UAE, Ghana	German, Pakistani and Italian
Child 2: Mikail	Emirati, German, Italian, Pakistani	Eurasian (mixed European and Asian descent)	Arabic, German, Italian, Urdu and English	Dubai, UAE, Ghana	German, Pakistani and Italian

CONVERSATION STARTERS

Here are a few conversation starters for you and your family to answer, perhaps over a weekend family dinner:

1. **A multicultural family is one that has more than one cultural influence inside the home or outside due to contact with the local community, or both. Are you a multicultural family?**

   - Take turns with each family member to discuss with which culture or cultures each of you identifies.
   - How do you balance the different cultural elements and expectations in your daily life?

2. **A multilingual family speaks either more than one language at home, or outside to communicate with its local community, or both. Are you a multilingual family?**

   - Take turns with each family member to discuss the language you feel strongest in and why?
   - Which language is your weakest and why?
   - Which language do you dream in?

3. **A multi-mobile family is one that has moved homes more than once (internationally or domestically or a combination of both). Are you a multi-mobile family?**

   - Take turns with each family member to discuss how each move has shaped you.
   - What has moving taught you about yourself?

4. **Are you a combination of two or more aspects such as a multicultural and multi-mobile family, but not a multilingual family?**

   - Please discuss your own particular combination. How messy has this made your life?

Answering these questions will help you to identify and focus on the MOLA parts most relevant for your family throughout the book.

CHAPTER TWO

THE MULTICULTURAL FAMILY

· ·

THE FABRIC OF YOUR MOLA

*"When cultures bump into each other,
the blend is never, ever boring."*

Jerry Jones

MY MULTICULTURAL FAMILY

HEATHROW AIRPORT, LONDON, 2004:

I look visibly nervous when it's time to board my flight from London to Karachi. A kind-looking air hostess taps me on my shoulder and says with a smile, "You nervous to fly, hon? Just take a deep breath and you'll be fine!"

I smile back and thank her. I'm not nervous to fly, but as the airplane takes off I feel terrified of the task I have to undertake once I land in Karachi. I plan on telling my Pakistani parents that I am in love with the half-German, half-Italian boy I met at my British university this

33

year and that we would like to get married in a few years. This was not a conversation to have over the phone or email, so I am going home this summer to tell them face to face. I am preparing myself for their reaction.

Are my Pakistani parents going to be shocked? Are they going to try to talk me out of my relationship, citing the huge cultural, religious and racial divide? What if they threaten to disown me? Or perhaps cut me off financially? Or are they going to prevent me from going back to the United States to finish up my senior year of college in the fall? Or prohibit me from ever seeing him again? Or insist that I was too young to be thinking of marriage? Or perhaps try to arrange a marriage for me with a Pakistani boy instead?

As the plane flies over the Arabian Sea, I play each of these scenarios in my head repeatedly and feverishly rehearse my lines. My parents have been incredibly supportive of my dreams and have spent much of their hard-earned money to send me to college in the United States and the United Kingdom. By Pakistani standards, they are liberal parents, who encourage me to live abroad independently and pursue a career in business. But am I pushing the envelope too far by falling in love with someone who comes from a different country and culture? Someone who is not Pakistani, doesn't speak my native tongue of Urdu and is not even a Muslim? There is no way to predict their reaction to my multicultural relationship.

As my plane touches down in the City of Lights, I feel a deep sense of anguish mixed with a feeling of joy and happiness to be back on home soil. I step onto the tarmac and feel that first burst of heat and humidity that is synonymous with home. Inside the airport, there is chaos around me as hordes of people disregard the immigration queues and try to jump ahead of each other. The idyllic English seaside town of Brighton, where Martino and I met, suddenly feels miles away, as if it took place in a different world. I can feel the change that my surroundings prompt in me. In England, I am an independent, confident young female traveler. In Pakistan, I know the rules are different. I approach a porter and ask him to help carry my luggage through customs control. Asking him to help me carry my suitcase provides him with a job and a chance to earn money. Not for the first time in my life I feel like the perfect chameleon, changing my colors depending on which part of the world I'm in. Somehow the familiarity of being back on home turf gives me the confidence that I need but it also accentuates my trepidation.

My parents come to pick me up from the airport, overjoyed to see their 21-year-old daughter back at last. It has been almost a year since we've seen each other, and they are full of questions about University, my studies and plans for the summer. I take a day to get over jetlag and get back on Pakistan time. Then I find my mother. She is in the kitchen, holding a tray of ripe, juicy Sindhri mangoes, freshly delivered from my grandparents' farm. I am terrified of telling both my parents at once, so I first confide in Mummy.

She immediately stops cutting the mango in her hand and puts down the knife.

"What are you saying, Mariam? Do you want to marry this boy?" she asks.

At first there is shock. Disbelief. Blank stares. Total incomprehension. As my mother struggles to digest the news, I can see the worry, confusion and doubts on her face. I can also see the number one question in her mind: What will people think? In my extended Pakistani family, no one has married a non-Pakistani or a non-Muslim. Culture, race and religion are three huge stumbling blocks that have ensured no one crosses this threshold. How would my grandparents react? My mother knows the accusations that will fly her way:

"You were too liberal in raising your daughter!"

"See, this is what happens when you send girls to study abroad!"

Despite her doubts, and to her credit, my mother hears me out, agrees to support me and shares the news with my father. He surprises both of us by remaining calm and asking questions about what Martino does, where he comes from, where his parents come from, what he is studying at university, how old he is and other personal and family details. Never one to care what society or extended family thinks, my father's main thought is: Is this the right person for my daughter? Finally, he takes off his glasses, turns to me and asks:

"Mariam, how can you thrive in a multicultural marriage and raise your future children with someone from the other corner of the world, with whom you have nothing in common? Your mother and I are extremely worried about what you're getting yourself into..."

"Daddy, I won't be the first person in the world to do it! Our plan is to learn as much as we can about each other before we get married and then decide how to raise a family in a way that works for both of us. And we have plenty of things in common, if you look past the obvious things. I know our backgrounds are very different, but we want the same things from life, going ahead in the future. And we need your support."

My parents share a concerned look but remain surprisingly calm. After many, many more questions and pieces of advice they give me their full support and encourage me to get to know Martino as well as his parents before we rush into marriage. They point out that we are both still quite young at 21 and 23, and we should use the next couple of years to learn as much as we can about each other's cultures, languages and families. Since our time in England has come to an end, we are to do this via a long-distance relationship, with me in Boston, and Martino back in Berlin as we finish up our degrees.

I've said goodbye to Martino in London, not knowing if I'd ever see him again and suddenly I feel a huge weight lift off my shoulders. I can't wait to tell him the good news! Later that evening as I go shopping to one of the local bazaars, I watch a shopkeeper as he measures out six yards of a beautiful turquoise-blue fabric and spins it together in his hands. With a sharp slice of the scissors, he then hands it to the customer in front of him and declares, "With such a beautiful basis, you don't need too many embellishments because the fabric itself will shine through."

I think to myself excitedly about the fabric I am weaving together and the cultures I am mixing together. I hope we too will end up with a beautiful result. But nothing has prepared me for the challenges that lie ahead. Nobody has taught me the rules of mixing cultures, so it is time to teach myself.

MULTICULTURALISM AS THE FABRIC OF YOUR MOLA

Your multicultural background forms the basis of your mola. Therefore, think of your multicultural background as the fabric of your mola. It is the basis of your design, so it needs to be a solid material upon which you design the rest of your mola. Which fabric best suits your mola? Is it smooth and shiny as silk and slippery to hold? Is it soft like cotton or rough like denim?

In identifying the fabric of a MOLA Family, I include three important components of multiculturalism – culture, race and religion – under the same umbrella because these factors are strongly interrelated. The mola you are trying to build as a MOLA Family will be better, prettier and more cohesive if you try to consciously incorporate all the different fabrics that make up your family.

CULTURE

According to the Merriam-Webster dictionary, culture is "the customary beliefs, social forms and material traits of a racial, religious or social group." It is "a set of shared attitudes, values, goals and practices."

Why does culture matter?

"Culture impacts our hearts," explains Trisha Carter, an interculturalist and organizational psychologist who works at the Cultural Intelligence Collective in Sydney, Australia, to help individuals and corporations increase their Cultural Intelligence (CQ). Culture is the prism through which we view the world, and in international families, culture plays a vital role in determining how we present ourselves to the outside world but also how we view others.

"Culture matters. It shapes us and molds us in ways we aren't consciously aware. The things our families and friends believe have impacted us and our beliefs and values. Often these are things we don't question but assume that it's what everyone believes. We think it's the 'right' way to behave. From the ways we address our elders, the ways we express appreciation, deal with conflict, communicate our wishes, plan for the future, choose our partners, raise our children, approach illness and death – all of these and many more are influenced by our cultures," explains Trisha.

Culture is driven by many factors, such as race, nationality, ethnicity and religion. In some ways, culture is the outcome of the interplay of all these elements. Culture can become an issue when we least expect it. Even if both partners live a similar life and have a similar outlook, we cannot deny our roots as these may guide our behavior. If you brush a certain culture under the rug you are not acknowledging that this is what your family is ultimately made up of. If you disregard culture you are cutting out certain fabrics from your mola.

> **"Culture matters. It shapes us and molds us in ways we aren't consciously aware. The things our families and friends believe have impacted us and our beliefs and values."**
>
> **— Trisha Carter.**

It is helpful to use the iceberg analogy, where culture is often compared to an iceberg that has both visible (on the surface) and invisible (below the surface) parts. Some behaviors are visible and above the water line such as the food we eat or the clothes we wear, but the biggest chunk of the iceberg is below the waterline, which consists of thinking and feeling, beliefs and values, needs and fears, all of which are culturally driven and often hidden beneath the surface. Hence, we must consciously 'lower the water line' to make those cultural aspects visible and really understand what drives our behavior.

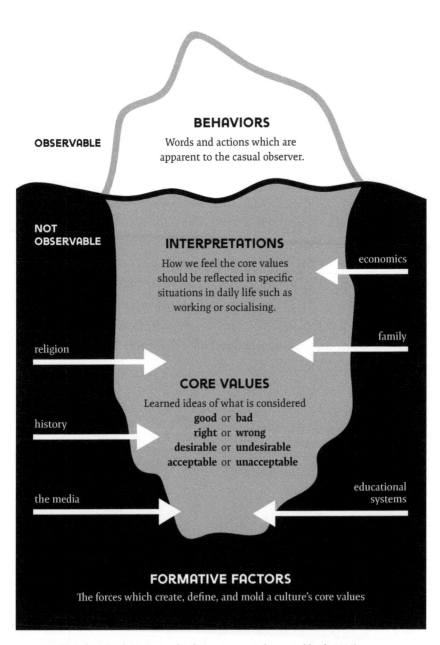

Figure 4: The Iceberg Analogy (copyrighted Language & Culture Worldwide 2015)

All the cultural influences in your family add up to one unique culture for your MOLA Family. If you don't sew your culture into your family design, you would not be able to agree on anything.

If you disregard culture, you are cutting out certain fabrics from your mola.

RACE

Race is different from culture in its narrowest definition, but it can be one of the most visible aspects, especially in a multiracial family. Race can also be a deceiving factor, as a multiracial family can be from a fairly similar cultural background (for example, both a white and a black person may identify as American), but even in that case, distinctive sub-cultures do exist which are linked to racial legacies and identities.

A biracial or multiracial family may arise due to a marriage or it may arise due to the adoption of children from a different race. In both these scenarios, a family may struggle to incorporate their different races, and their children may struggle to identify with one or the other.

"Anyone raising kids cross-culturally shares a core set of challenges. Adoption adds a layer that not all families deal with. It comes with a unique set of challenges and opportunities," explains Jerry Jones.

RELIGION

Religion and culture are closely related, yet in many ways are very much apart. Even people with the same religious background (for example, a Moroccan and an Indonesian Muslim, or a European and an African Christian) may face huge cultural differences. In such cases, a common religion may erroneously downplay cultural differences and cause misunderstandings.

"Don't take for granted what you know about culture. Culture is complex and crossing cultures and religions even more so. Learn as much as you can about this because its relevance lasts a lifetime," advises intercultural strategist Sundae Schneider-Bean, who provides coaching to individuals and organizations to cross cultures effectively.

Different religious traditions in the same family need to be addressed, as they are drivers of cultures and behaviors and form part of family history and legacy, both within the core family but even more so when interacting with the extended family. Outright denial of any of these religious traditions is likely to cause friction and unresolved grief, so each family needs to decide for itself to what degree it wishes to honor these different traditions but needs to understand that they cannot (and perhaps even should not) simply be erased.

These are the core aspects that influence your multicultural family and form the fabric of your mola.

DEFINITIONS AND EXAMPLES OF MULTICULTURAL FAMILIES

What does a multicultural family look like? A multicultural family is one that has more than one cultural influence inside or outside the home due to contact with the local community, or both because of its globally mobile lifestyle. A multicultural family may also be multi-ethnic, multi-religious or multi-racial, although not necessarily.

"As parents raising a cross-cultural family, we have a stupefying amount of power to shape the way our children see the world and themselves.

Although it is well-known that speaking the native language(s) at home helps pass on culture(s) to your children, less attention is given to the role of communication. Yet, we know from social scientific research that communication is how we explain and make sense of our experiences. It is also how we make sense of who we are, our identity," explains Sundae.

She highlights that multicultural families must be mindful of their communication and what they are shaping. In particular, Sundae advises parents: "Pay special attention to how you talk about your family's respective cultures," asking:

- Is there an inherent 'us' vs 'them' or competitive quality present?

- Do you talk about your partner's culture(s) as positively as you do your own?

- Do you both openly discuss drawbacks and celebrate each culture's positive influence?

Sundae further advises: "Give your children a range of language to talk about their own identities," asking:

- Do you expose your children to language and imagery that normalizes a cross-cultural life (i.e. through books, images, or films featuring biracial, multiracial or interreligious families, and stories about or by Cross-Cultural or Third-Culture Kids)?

- Do you allow your children to explore those identities and discover what feels like a 'fit' for them at that time?

"As parents, we have the opportunity through the way we communicate to co-create how our children see culture, themselves, and their cross-cultural family. Choose your strategies wisely," advises Sundae.

"Give your children a range of language to talk about their own identities."
— Sundae Schneider-Bean

MEET THE MOLA FAMILIES

There are many examples of multicultural families living around the world. These categories arose from research I conducted through *The Mobile Family Survey* in 2018:

A Cross-Cultural Family Who Moves

Rachel is from Scotland, while her husband is from the Faroe Islands (which belong to Denmark). They are a cross-cultural family who have raised their three Scottish-Danish children in Scotland, the UAE and the United States. They are a multicultural family due to their different cultures both at home and outside the home.

"One of the additional challenges our family faces is when there is a disagreement over a move," explains Rachel.

A Cross-Cultural Family Who Has Not Moved

Maria's family is a multicultural family, combining both Chinese and American cultures at home. Her family is not a mobile family in that they have not moved internationally, but their cross-cultural background at home makes them a multicultural family.

"My kids are half Chinese-American and half Caucasian. We live in a suburb of New York with very few Asians. Because the non-Chinese culture is so dominant, I fear my children will not identify enough with their Chinese culture and that heritage will be lost," says Maria.

A Monocultural Family Who Moves

Michelle and her husband are both Australian, so they started off as a monocultural family at home. All three of their children were born in Australia, but they have been moving internationally for the past few years and have lived in the UAE, Oman and Malaysia. Their children have adopted many aspects from their host countries' cultures, and today their family culture is a strong mix of their native Australian culture and those of their adopted countries.

"Socially acceptable behavior towards children in some cultures makes my children feel uncomfortable, especially when they stand out from the local people," says Michelle.

A Multiracial Family Through Adoption Who Moves

Louisa and her husband are both Canadian with three biological children, but they adopted two children while living in Mexico as expats. They have lived in the United States, Canada and Mexico.

"We raise our five children equally, based on what we believe to be best for them, but sometimes we will receive comments from those in our host country (Mexico) about what we should be doing with our two Mexican children," says Louisa.

A Multi-religious Family Who Moves

Hiba and her husband are both Lebanese expats living in the UAE. They are the same nationality but belong to two different religions: Christianity and Islam. They are raising their children in Dubai with exposure to both of their religious backgrounds.

"My husband and I come from different backgrounds and religions. This has impacted our relationship and how we want to raise our kids," says Hiba.

THE CHALLENGES AND OPPORTUNITIES OF A MULTICULTURAL FAMILY – OUR EXPERTS ADVISE

Being a multicultural family, regardless of type (dealing with culture, race, religion or a combination of the above) brings forth its own unique challenges and opportunities. I collected data from hundreds of international families through *The Mobile Family Survey* in 2018, through which participants shared their experiences from around the world. I chose a few examples of the challenges faced by multicultural families and asked my team of three intercultural experts to offer some advice and solutions.

White Parents Raising Adopted Black Kids in South Africa

Svenja was born in Germany, while her husband was born in South Africa. As a couple, they have lived in the UK and in South Africa and their two children were both born in South Africa.

"My partner and I are both white, but our adopted children are black. As much as we try, in post-Apartheid South Africa where the racial divide is still huge, it is not easy to connect our children with their birth culture and instill a strong sense of identity in them," explains Svenja.

However, this cross-cultural and multi-racial family also enjoys many opportunities.

"Experiencing diversity is one of the most important opportunities for us, as we want to teach our girls that there is so much beauty and richness in diversity. We want them to feel proud of being part of a diverse family, a diverse circle of friends and diverse cultures."

○ ○ ○

Q: HOW CAN SVENJA INSTILL A STRONG SENSE OF IDENTITY IN HER MULTICULTURAL FAMILY THAT ENCAPSULATES THEIR DIVERSITY?

A: Expert Jerry Jones has some advice for Svenja on blending cultures:

Dear Svenja,

The ability to process all sides is a critical skill for global people. Some parts of the global life are just not good. Trying to veil them with positives creates a false narrative. There is no way to look on the bright side of racism, bigotry or hatred. However, that never negates the reality that positives exist in the same space and at the same time.

First and foremost, keep your kids safe. Believe them. Advocate for them. Protect them.

Create safe spaces for them to share their deepest concerns and work hard not to transfer your own bias. Children are constantly processing the world around them, but they may not be thinking what you think they are. You may be shocked to learn that what bothers you most is not even a stressor for them. At the same time, you may be equally shocked to discover what their fears actually are. Take care of the monsters under the bed before you fix the remnants of Apartheid.

Seek out unlikely heroes. There is something rich about hearing the stories of people who cherish respect and diversity even though they were taught something completely different. Find people whose hearts have been dramatically changed over time and let them pour into your kids.

Model grace. Not naivete. Not ignorance. Not blind, unchecked forgiveness. Just grace. Choose to take a higher road than the offensive people around you, not because it will teach them a lesson. Extend grace because it changes things at the core.

Best,

Jerry

British Mother and Egyptian ATCK Father Raise Children as Muslims in Dubai

Rachel D is British, while her husband is an Egyptian ATCK who was born and raised in the UAE. Currently raising their own two boys in Dubai, Rachel explains that as a multicultural family, religion is something they are constantly navigating.

"We are from different religious upbringings and this will always be a challenge as it manifests itself in different ways, especially when raising children. For example, celebrating Christmas: we always celebrate Islamic holidays such as Ramadan and Eid, but my husband didn't want to have a Christmas tree because he felt it would confuse the boys as we're raising them Muslim. I've told my husband how important it is to me to decorate the house including having a Christmas tree, and this year he bought us two for the house. We are slowly learning how to find ways to celebrate both of our backgrounds, whilst ensuring we raise our boys as Muslim and they are clear about their faith," explains Rachel D.

In spite of the challenges, Rachel D is appreciative of how her children have access to other cultures.

"Being married to someone from a different country, religion and culture has broadened my outlook, made me more tolerant and taught me to find ways to communicate with people from different backgrounds, on a personal and professional level. I hope this will be the same for our children and I love how they easily adapt and enjoy three different cultures: Emirati, British and Egyptian, which has enriched our lives immensely!" she says.

o o o

Q: HOW CAN RACHEL CONTINUE TO COMMUNICATE EFFECTIVELY IN HER FAMILY TO CREATE A FAMILY CULTURE THAT INCORPORATES THEIR DIVERSE UPBRINGING?

A: Expert Sundae Schneider-Bean has some advice for Rachel and multicultural families like hers:

Dear Rachel,

In your multicultural family, two religious traditions adjoin. While you seem to support raising your children as Muslim, you also make it clear that you do not want all your Christian religious traditions to be erased. Here is what I think is working for you:

There is alignment on the faith-based traditions your children will follow.

Rachel, you are in the minority from a faith perspective and have expressed what specific aspects of your traditions are important to have space in your family culture.

Your partner is willing to experiment with incorporating other cultural traditions in the family structure.

You recognize both the challenges and the immense benefits of raising a family in a multicultural context.

As a family, you have found a way to incorporate both religious backgrounds in a way that is in alignment with *your* needs. A unique third culture is created as a result, where your children are raised Muslim, yet exposed to Christian traditions.

Couples in similarly complex multicultural families could benefit from:

- Individually reflecting on which cultural, religious, language or other practices are most important to you, then sharing these with your partner.

- Aligning as a couple on which practices will contribute to a family culture that you both embrace.

- Experimenting with how these practices can be creatively integrated into your family routines and traditions.

When tackling the challenges of raising a multicultural family, focus first on your core needs, then get creative on how you can get these needs met.

Best,
Sundae.

An ATCK and a CCK Raise Children in a Mixed Religion Family in Bahrain

Jordana is an ATCK who was born in Bahrain and holds three nationalities: Lebanese, British and Australian. Her CCK husband who was also born in Bahrain, holds Iraqi and Bahraini nationalities. They currently live in Bahrain with their two kids.

"Raising children in a mixed religion household is very difficult as some ideas of the other's religion are hard to get on board with. We haven't overcome this, we just try as much as possible to have a solid foundation on what we believe religion to be," explains Jordana.

She also listed her families mixed religious and cultural background as a huge advantage in terms of raising their children.

"Because we are one of the few families that are this mixed, I always try and emphasize to my kids that everyone may be different, but we are all made the same, we all look at the same sky and the same stars, so it doesn't matter what is on the outside," she continues.

o o o

Q: HOW CAN JORDANA COMMUNICATE EFFECTIVELY TO ENSURE THAT HER MULTI-RELIGIOUS FAMILY BACKGROUND CONTINUES TO BE AN ADVANTAGE AND NOT A PROBLEM?

A: **Expert Trisha Carter has some communication advice for Jordana and multicultural families like hers:**

Dear Jordana,

You are beginning from a point of significant strength because you are viewing the religious and cultural mixes that your family brings together as a 'huge advantage' and are encouraging your children to see the common humanity in everyone. I totally agree with you, but I know others who would see the challenges first and be limited by this mindset.

To value and appreciate the differences places you in a great position to discuss with your husband (and him with you) the ideas that are more difficult to get on board with. You will continue to benefit from communicating your own religious beliefs and experiences to each other with openness and curiosity. Asking "I wonder why..." will help take that open and curious stance and will support ongoing discussion which is critical.

Find the points of agreement and celebrate those. Make a list of common beliefs. These will be an anchor to return to if the difficult ideas become a point of discomfort or conflict.

Open discussion will set the tone for the children to continue to learn and accept the differences. For them, it may initially be more about holidays and rituals and less about difficult ideas.

What holidays will we celebrate and how? What rituals are important as a family? Getting clear on expectations and comfort levels will make it easier to communicate with extended family and friends. The children can be encouraged to see themselves as 'lucky' as they can enjoy more holidays!

Best,
Trisha.

Most interviewees highlighted that while they continued to face numerous challenges in raising their multicultural families, from what to name their children to differences in cultural practices, they were also able to appreciate the richness in experience, exposure and environment it provided for their family.

YOUR MOLA TOOLBOX: M IS FOR MIX

So how did I move from that terrified 21-year-old to a confident 35-year-old wife and mother of two, who knows and understands what makes her multicultural family tick?

I stopped fearing the mess. I allowed things to get as confusing as possible. And then I became good at mixing. Mixing cultures, religions and races to produce our own unique blend of a multicultural family. Somedays I felt like a scientist, other days an artist. The more I mixed, the more unique combinations I came up with. To this day, I think nothing of serving an Italian appetizer, a Pakistani main course and a German dessert! In my mind, together they create a unique dinner menu, although I am sure I have startled dinner guests with my multi-ethnic, fusion food combinations on many an occasion. Like that marble cake, I never know which combination of swirls will come out once I've placed it in the oven.

Therefore, in my framework of a MOLA Family, M stands for Mix. The first rule of creating a MOLA Family is to start mixing the various cultures, races and religions that you and your partner bring to the table.

MIXING CULTURES

So how can multicultural families start mixing their diverse cultures to form their own unique family culture? Firstly, you need to include your home cultures as well as the cultures of where you have lived or grown up. For me, this meant including certain elements of Pakistani and American cultures, the two countries I have lived in predominantly. You then need to include the cultures where your partner comes from and has grown up in. For my husband, this meant including German and Italian culture. Then you need to add your children to the mix and include the cultures they grew up in too, due to your globally mobile lifestyle. For us this meant including Singaporean and UAE culture. On any given day, our family is mixing six distinct cultures!

Every MOLA Family creates its own family culture, which is a combination of different elements of its various cultural influences. Our family culture is thus a mish-mash of all of the above. We are cultural chameleons; we like to breakfast on spicy South Asian omelets one day and dark rye German bread with cheese the next. Our formal attire includes suede boots and *sarees* (not worn together!), our conversations at the dining table flow from German, to English, to Urdu, and on long car drives through the UAE, our kids sing songs and nursery rhymes in Italian and Arabic. We eat with our hands, use chopsticks or eat with a fork and knife depending on what we're eating. We use our various cultures to form some common family values: respect for elders (Pakistani), encourage independence in our children from a young age (German) and make sure food is a family affair and enjoyed together (Italian). Other family values include respecting diversity, not making fun of people with accents in one language and making friends from all around the world. Our favorite family activities are travel, reading books and exploring our host city.

We try to actively recognize what part of our culture is driving our behavior and when we disagree on a topic (which is the norm rather than the exception), we take off our defensive hats and put on our listening hats. We resolve differences by listening to each other and then figuring out how we can deal with a challenge that incorporates who we both are.

For example, when my son Mikail had difficulty adjusting to another child in his kindergarten group, my immediate solution was to involve his teachers and seek their help. As a South Asian, I tend to put my trust in reaching out to an authority to resolve an issue. Martino thought it was better to let the kids sort it out themselves and not make too big a deal out of it. As a German, he thinks it's important to encourage young children to become problem solvers which helps them to learn how to get along with different people. In the end, we decided to first try his approach and then try mine if we needed extra help.

We try to actively recognize what part of our culture is driving our behavior and when we disagree on a topic (which is the norm rather than the exception), we take off our defensive hats and put on our listening hats.

MIXING RACES

If you are a biracial or multiracial family like us, it is important to address the different races present in your family. When our daughter Mina was five years old, she asked us out of the blue at breakfast, "Mama why are you brown, but Papa is white? And what does that make me?"

I grabbed the nearest box of eggs from our kitchen counter and showed her how some eggs were brown on the outside while others were white. Then we cracked open one egg from each. As the egg white and yolk spilled out of each, she turned to me with a smile and said, "From the inside, they're both the same!"

"Exactly Mina, exactly. You are both brown and white, but in the end, we're all the same from the inside."

It is important to acknowledge race and help a child feel comfortable with their mixed heritage, but as a parent it is equally important to show that regardless of race, we are all similar on the inside.

However, be prepared that race is an ongoing discussion in most multicultural families. About a year later, Mina came back to me and declared, "I am white, right, Mama?" A child's sense of identity is forever developing and forming. As a parent I find it is important to continue the discussion and keep channels of communication open. Just having this discussion once with a child is never enough – be prepared to have it many times in different shapes and forms as your child grows older. The most important factor is to encourage communication on this topic from an early age, so that your child always feels comfortable to talk to you about his or her identity and race.

> **"Race is an ongoing discussion in most multicultural families. Just having this discussion once with a child is never enough – be prepared to have it many times in different shapes and forms as your child grows older."**

MIXING RELIGIONS

This is probably the toughest mix to achieve. Each multicultural family must find a way that works best for them. My best advice is to keep in mind three essential elements: balance, compromise and the realization that your solutions may not be a one-size-fits-all.

For my particular family, this was a tough balance to achieve. One of the major controversial topics in Islamic research and discourse is whether a Muslim woman can marry a non-Muslim man. As a Muslim woman, I faced major issues with marrying a non-Muslim man, even though Martino was a Christian. In Islam, Christians and Jews are recognized as 'People of the Book' but while a Muslim man can marry a Christian or a Jewish female, a Muslim woman cannot marry a Christian or a Jewish man. Conservative Islamic theologists cite their reasons, while liberal interpretations of the Quranic text argue that Muslim women should be given the same marriage rights as Muslim men.

Theological debates aside, this stark reality gave us sleepless nights, as it meant that if I married Martino, our marriage would not be recognized in Islam, or in my home country of Pakistan.

I did not want to pressure Martino to convert to Islam. I loved him as he was and felt we had a commonality of faith which bonded us together. We both felt more spiritual than religious. Living abroad for many years had made me re-evaluate which religious practices I followed because I truly believed in them and which practices I only followed because society deemed them as acceptable rituals. I learned to keep the former and let go of the latter. Ironically, this had strengthened my faith.

My parents were prepared to accept Martino for who he was too. But they knew that it would be a lot easier for my grandparents and extended family to accept Martino if he accepted Islam.

"Has the boy accepted Islam?" asked Nani Amma, my maternal grandmother in Pakistan.

"Not yet," answered my mother.

"Leave it in *Allah's* hands," replied Nani Amma.

My parents kept shielding me from my grandparents' questions during this time. By virtue of distance, I was spared any direct pressure. In the end, I felt it was not my decision to make. I did not want to start my marriage by forcing my husband to be anything that he was not. Rather, I wanted us to agree on how we would raise our future children together.

For almost two years we discussed the topic of our different religions and how to mix them. During these two years Martino did as much research and learning about Islam as possible. Some days there were no easy answers. Martino took the decision out of my hands one day by going to a mosque in Berlin and reciting the one sentence, the *kalima*, that makes one a Muslim: "I believe there is only one God and that Muhammad is his last messenger." He then phoned me in South Hadley, Massachusetts, where I was completing my senior year at Mount Holyoke College to tell me he had officially accepted Islam.

I was sitting in my dorm room and was just about to go to a lecture. It was November in New England and the snow flurries were gently falling outside. Soon the entire college campus would be covered in snow, just in time for the Thanksgiving holiday.

I remember being stunned into silence, staring out at the snow.

"Mariam, are you still there?" asked Martino.

My stunned reaction was probably not the one Martino had been hoping for. I was upset. Relieved. Furious. Hopeful. I didn't know whether to cry or to congratulate him. I knew he had done it to make our marriage easily accepted, and I knew he had done it for me.

"Yeah. I'm just so shocked. Are you sure? I don't want you to regret this? Or resent me for it..." My voice trailed off.

While I was grateful to him for trying to pave the way for our married life together, I also wanted us to stay true to who we were. So, I made a pact with him that day. Yes, his acceptance of Islam meant that we could get married in a mosque, have an Islamic marriage certificate and have our marriage recognized in my home country. But I still wanted to raise our children in a multicultural household. We agreed we would raise our children in a way that honored and respected their diverse heritage and cultures. How to get this balance right was up to us to figure out.

Martino's parents, my lovely parents-in-law living in Germany, were upset at first. They felt they were losing their only son to a religion foreign to them. We had many discussions by phone, email and in person together. I wanted to have an open and honest dialogue with them about what this meant for our future.

"Please don't change your name to a Muslim one," implored Martino's mother. They had named him Martino as part of a Sicilian tradition where the new generations carry on the name of their paternal grandfathers. Apart from the family history, the name Martino in Italian tradition comes from St. Martino; a saint who shared his coat with a freezing beggar in front of the city gates. The name thus means someone who is compassionate and fights injustice and inequality.

We had done our research and consulted Imams in both Boston and Berlin and reassured Martino's parents that he did not need to change his name.

It helped when we all met together in Germany over the winter holidays in Martino's hometown of Wolfsburg, Germany. Martino turned to both of his parents and said, "Look at me. I'll always be your son. Exactly the son you raised. This will never change."

I truly believe that had my parents-in-law not extended their full support to us during this time, our relationship may have crumbled. My German mother-in-law, and my Italian father-in-law, who had already accepted me into their family, understood that we had to pave our own way into our cross-cultural marriage. I remember the moment so clearly when Salvatore, my Italian father-in-law-to-be, stood in the kitchen of their Wolfsburg house, leaning against the counter. The smell of rich German coffee was brewing while the fresh bread just out of the oven filled the air and made my mouth water.

"We found our way to make it work, Marlies, now let them find theirs," he said to his wife.

When it came to mixing our multicultural family together, Martino and I were blessed to have the support of all four parents. Discussions, debates and decisions were never easy, but we worked through them from a place of love and mutual respect. In return, the joy of watching our two families connect and create a bond that surpasses continents, cultures, races, religions and languages has been the most enriching experience for us all. I truly hope that one day I can be as good a parent to my children as my parents and my parents in law have been for us – they are my role models and biggest sources of inspiration.

HOW TO MIX YOUR FABRICS

Every MOLA Family needs to figure out a technique for mixing their multicultural identities. The basic premise is not to just randomly mix, but to wholeheartedly understand and embrace the different cultural influences through constant communication, dialogue and exposure.

It is important to highlight that not every fabric in your mola needs to be equal – some can and should be more dominant than others and figure more prominently, while others can be of a more secondary or tertiary nature. In this sense, different cultural influences are given different statuses and 'degrees of importance', but this can only happen through dialogue and agreement. No cultural influence should be (willingly or unwillingly) subjugated or negated, as this may threaten the very essence of the mola.

It is also helpful to remember that a mola is a living, dynamic piece of clothing, so the fabrics may and will change over time or be replaced by others. Your MOLA Family is a continuous work in progress.

THE FIVE RULES FOR MULTICULTURAL (MIXED) FAMILIES

1. SOLUTIONS WILL NOT BE A ONE-SIZE-FITS-ALL AND REQUIRE PATIENCE AND AN ABILITY TO COMPROMISE

Multicultural families need to get creative with their solutions. They may find that a one-size-fits-all solution does not apply to them and so thinking outside the box is a key skill for multicultural families to develop. For instance, in our family we agreed that our kids would be exposed to both their cultural heritages, and so our children celebrate Christmas with their European grandparents and Eid with their South Asian grandparents. We are raising them with exposure to both the East and the West and hoping to shape them as bridging that cultural divide; both culturally and linguistically.

2. SEEK NEUTRAL GROUND ON COMPLEX ISSUES

This may sound counterproductive and counterintuitive in terms of adding more complexity, but seeking neutral ground on complex issues such as which religion to follow (yours or mine?) or which country or city to raise your family in (yours, mine or another?), can help you maintain a healthy balance in your multicultural family. For example, we sought neutral ground in terms of where to raise our family. Cities such as Copenhagen, Singapore and Dubai, have suited us much better than Berlin, Milan or Karachi. The pressure to conform to one particular culture is always greater when we have lived in one of our home countries. Which is why living on neutral ground, in 'expatland', has helped us to expose our children to their different cultural heritage and helped to maintain a balance between our different cultures. Living on neutral ground means you both work hard at maintaining your cultural ties, without taking them for granted. Living on neutral ground is not possible for every multicultural family but seeking a neutral approach to making big decisions in respect to your family life is possible.

3. CREATE YOUR OWN TRADITIONS, RULES AND A FAMILY IDENTITY

Each MOLA Family must create its own set of rules, values and traditions that ultimately form its family identity and shape its family culture. For example, one of our core family cultural elements is that we celebrate holidays and events by traveling and taking our kids to see a new place. Experiencing new countries and cultures helps to reinforce the diversity present inside the home and outside. We also borrow heavily from the culture of the country we happen to be living in - for example we have incorporated celebrating Chinese New Year into our family culture after living in Singapore, and after living in the UAE our children ask to eat Arabic/Middle Eastern food at least once a week.

4. LET YOUR CHILDREN MAKE UP THEIR OWN MINDS AS TO WHO THEY ARE

Sometimes the hardest thing for multicultural families to accept is that their children will have a rather different upbringing from their own. As parents, we all struggle with passing on our roots to our children, while raising them in a country and culture perhaps different than our own. For us, this struggle becomes more apparent each year when our children are asked to dress up for 'International Day' at their school in Dubai. The first year Mina insisted on dressing up in a Chinese cheongsam because she felt she came from Singapore – the country where she was born and initially grew up in. I respected her decision and sent her dressed in a Chinese dress. A few years later and she feels she comes from Dubai, so it is important to recognize a child's attachment to the places they are growing up in as opposed to the culture (s) that their parents hail from.

5. LET FOOD BRING YOU CLOSER

Never underestimate the importance and role food can play in bridging cultures. Food is a great way for a multicultural family to express who they are and share a part of their cultural roots, while also respecting the diversity in their backgrounds and experiences. One of my best examples of food helping to bring my family closer is through eating rice. Rice, which is a staple in so many cultures and cuisines, is cooked so differently throughout the world. In Pakistani or South Asian cuisine, rice is supposed to be cooked to perfection and be long, fluffy, easily separable, not stuck together and the longer the grain the better. But in Italian cooking, rice is frequently cooked 'al dente' as in risotto which is creamy, sticky, and short. This shows me how two cultures can look at the same ingredient and use it so differently and have such different expectations of how it should look and taste! Learning to eat rice in its many shapes and forms reminds us that we may perceive the same thing in a completely different way and encourages us to keep an open mind.

CHAPTER SUMMARY

1. Your multicultural background is the fabric of your MOLA Family. Culture, race and religion can all form part of your multicultural fabric.

2. Multicultural families may be formed due to a cross-cultural marriage, through adoption, or through leading a globally mobile life.

3. Some of the biggest challenges faced by multicultural families involve blending their different races, religions and cultures together. But the best opportunities enjoyed by multicultural families include experiencing diversity firsthand and adopting a global outlook.

4. In your MOLA toolbox, M stands for mix. In creating a MOLA Family, it is important for multicultural families to mix their different nationalities, cultures, races and religions through constant communication, dialogue and exposure.

5. To mix your multicultural family, it is important to recognize there might not be a one-size-fits-all approach, search for neutral ground on complex issues, create your own unique family identity, give your children the freedom to form their own cross-cultural identities and use food to bridge culture gaps.

ACTIVITY: WHICH CULTURES ARE PRESENT IN YOUR MOLA FAMILY?

Let's explore the different cultural influences in your family. These could be cultures present in your family and also your interaction with the culture of your host country.

1. **Which cultural influences are present in your family as a result of your multicultural family and globally mobile lifestyle?**

2. **Where do these cultural influences overlap/reinforce each other?**

3. **Where do these cultural influences differ and potentially clash?**

4. What are the most pivotal challenges you face as a multicultural family?

5. In what situation do you choose culture as the best way forward and why?

6. What family culture has arisen out of the outcomes of your blended MOLA Family?

FOR INSPIRATION, HERE ARE SOME OF MY ANSWERS:

1. **Which cultural influences are present in your family as a result of your multicultural family and globally mobile lifestyle?**

   Our cultural influences are:
   - Pakistani
   - German
   - Italian
   - American
   - Emirati
   - Singaporean
   - Danish
   - Ghanaian

2. **When do your cultures overlap?**

   - Italian and Pakistani: family, food, respect for elders
   - German and Singaporean: efficiency, propriety, following rules
   - Italian and American: spontaneity, creativity
   - Ghanaian and Pakistani: traditionalism, rituals, superstitions and the role of women. Both cultures are matriarchal cultures.

3. **When do your cultures clash?**

   German and Pakistani cultures clash on just about everything: parenting styles, parenting approaches, expectations of schools and authorities, extended family expectations, household duties, having household help.

4. What are the challenges you face as a multicultural family?

Our biggest challenge is trying to find the 'middle ground' between different cultural expectations when it comes to fundamental issues such as how to raise children. Our parenting style is constantly criticized for either being 'too protective' (by German standards) or 'not careful enough' (by Pakistani standards). Everything from how we dress our kids, to how much freedom we allow them is interpreted differently in German and Pakistani cultures. Our challenge has been to do what makes us comfortable and not necessarily what conforms to society's expectations of us as parents.

5. In what situation do you choose culture as the best way forward and why?

When it comes to disagreements, we try to understand the reason why. If it seems cultural, we try to detect the reason(s) behind the disagreement and then decide on the objectively more sensible approach.

6. What family culture has arisen out of the outcomes of your blended MOLA Family?

Our family culture that has arisen from our different cultures is individualistic. We do things only if they make sense to us both. We don't follow rituals and traditions 'just for the sake of it.' The only expectations that matter in our family are ours. When we are given advice from one set of extended family or the other, we listen politely and explain 'our way' which may be a culmination of our home cultures interacting with our host culture to create our unique blend. Living on neutral ground (not in any of our home countries) gives us that extra freedom to carve out our own family culture.

CONVERSATION STARTERS

Here are a few conversation starters for you and your family to answer, perhaps over a weekend family dinner:

1. **Your multicultural background is the fabric of your MOLA Family.**

    - Imagine a roll of fabric. What does your family fabric look like?
    - What color, material, texture and depth does your fabric have? And why? For example, if you choose cotton, why does cotton represent your MOLA Family? Is it because your MOLA is soft and breathable, since you embrace and absorb all your differences? Or perhaps the fabric of your MOLA Family is more linen because it is difficult to manufacture yet highly absorbent and helps you stay cool and comfortable in spite of any inhospitable climate you may encounter? Or perhaps the fabric of your MOLA Family is silk, because it is shimmery and impenetrable, beautiful to look at yet protective of the family underneath?

2. **Culture plays a part in food-related etiquette, and multicultural families are often used to eating different cuisines and in different ways.**

    - Ask your family members: where are you when you eat?

- Do you and your MOLA Family eat with a fork and knife? Do you eat with chopsticks and spoons? Or do you eat with your hands? If you eat with your hands, do you use only your right hand? Or does it depend on what you are eating?
- Is licking your fingers considered polite or is it considered impolite and only to be indulged in when no one is watching?
- Is leaving food on your plate considered offensive or polite?
- Do you use a napkin to wipe your face and fingers while eating or do you wait till you're finished and then wash your hands in a bowl of water or in the bathroom?

3. **Multicultural families often create their own traditions and holidays.**

- Ask your family members: what do you celebrate as a MOLA Family? Do you celebrate cultural, religious or national holidays? If so, which ones?
- What do these celebrations mean to you and your family? Why is it important for you to celebrate these with your family?

4. **Multicultural families use their different cultural influences to create their own set of values to live by.**

- Ask your family members: what are your basic family values and why?
- Why are particular values important to you?
- How do you encourage these values in your children and in your daily life?

CHAPTER THREE

THE MULTILINGUAL FAMILY

. . . .

THE THREAD OF YOUR MOLA

"Languages don't divide, they bring families together."

Rita Rosenback

MY MULTILINGUAL FAMILY

TANGLIN MALL, SINGAPORE, 2014:

"I want the booze! I want the booze! I waaaaaaaaaaaaant the booze!" screams my two-year-old daughter Mina as we are standing in the middle of the queue in one of Singapore's most crowded Starbucks. I take a quick look around the coffee shop and see the usual mix of students, mothers and a few business people all enjoying their coffee who are now looking up at me and my daughter quizzically.

I try to calm Mina down, who is still strapped in her pram, but frantically kicking up a fuss and pointing at what she wants behind the glass.

Before I can say or do anything else, the lady sporting short blonde hair and standing in the queue behind me taps my shoulder and asks with a half amused and half concerned look in a clear Australian accent: "Is your daughter asking you for booze?"

I wish at this moment the floor would just open up and swallow me whole. Oh, the embarrassment! What must she think? What must everyone think? Is everyone staring at me? Are they all judging me?

Feeling like I have just sunk to a new low in my journey as a multilingual parent, it takes all my effort to stay calm under the circumstances and respond to this woman:

"Yes, well, she is actually asking for some watermelon in my native language. You see, watermelon in Urdu is called 'tarbooze', except she can't pronounce the word properly since she's only two, so she calls it 'booze.' I assure you it's not what you think!"

Is my face red? Yes.

Are those not-so-silent judgment looks directed at me? Yes.

Does this lady believe me? Probably not.

#parentingfail.

"Ready to order, lah?" asks the bored teenage cashier with bright neon hair who is waiting impatiently for me to order. I order a big cup of sliced watermelon and my usual java chip mocha Frappuccino in this tropical heat, while trying to push the stroller, keep Mina in as she is struggling to get out, handing over some of their iconic green straws to distract her, while pulling out my wallet and trying to pay in one go. I know I probably look like the very picture of a harassed mother. This week, like many weeks in my expat life, I am solo parenting a willful toddler while Martino is away on business in Vietnam and Indonesia, trying to hold it all together and not lose the plot. My travel article for

Expat Living Singapore is overdue, I am behind on my editing work for the local lifestyle magazine that I work for and it looks like I'm also failing at multilingual parenthood. At this point the only thing that can help me get through the day is caffeine, which is why I have dragged myself over to Tanglin Mall.

To her credit, Mina is finally happy with her big cup of fresh fruit with lots of 'booze' a.k.a watermelon in it. The Australian lady sitting by the window gives me a wry smile. And I think to myself of the two most important lessons I have learned that day:

1. It is dangerous when your child mixes two languages to make a request which sounds absurd in one language and extremely concerning in another.

2. This is probably going to be the first of many hilarious stories I will accumulate as a parent trying to raise my multilingual kids.

Suddenly the absurdity of the situation makes me laugh. I shed a few good tears, as I hold Mina in my arms and find a table to sit at. Teaching her my native tongue of Urdu was never going to be easy. Am I prepared for more of these looks, uncomfortable situations and even more temper tantrums and rebellions? Being raised bilingually with Urdu and English means I constantly switch back and forth myself but I don't want to confuse my daughter. Do I only speak to her in Urdu? Or do I speak in the way that comes most naturally to me: a constant mix of Urdu and English interspersed together? Why can't I be more consistent in my language choice like Martino, who only speaks to Mina in German? He never mixes German with Italian, his other native tongue. Is it because he grew up with the 'One Person, One Language' rule and I grew up with the 'Minority Language at Home' rule, which later turned into 'you speak whichever language the situation requires'?

With four native languages between us, what is the best language model for our family? Where are all the books on how to decide which native language to pass on to your kids, when you have more than one yourself, your partner, too, has more than one, and you communicate with each other in yet another language? What happens when two bilingual people get married and raise their children with four or more languages? And what happens when they keep moving around the world and adding new languages to their family life?

I was tired of hearing and reading about the simple narratives where each parent had one language to impart to their children and easily came up with a clear, concise plan. Oh, how I envied them. And then here I was; choosing one language over another feels like I am denying part of who I am. Is it normal to feel this way? How does a bilingual parent 'let go' of one of their languages when it comes time to raise their own kids?

Choosing Urdu feels like the right but more difficult choice. Even while growing up in Pakistan, I attended a British school, so in a true colonial legacy, subjects like History, Mathematics and even Islamic Studies, were all conducted in English. Although I speak Urdu fluently, ask me to explain the solar system or World War 1 and I would have to revert to English because that is the academic language in which I have been taught. Adding to this is a complicating social reality. Pakistani society does not value speaking Urdu; all children are taught English as this is considered the language that the educated elite speaks. My sister speaks to her kids in English, not Urdu, as do most of my cousins living in Karachi.

Choosing English would be the easier choice, but then where would Mina learn Urdu? Definitely not from her German/Italian father. Her Pakistani grandparents live in Pakistan – a seven-hour flight from Singapore – and even they mix constantly between Urdu and English. And yet the thought of Mina not speaking or understanding any Urdu broke my heart at first. For the first time ever, I understood that language is not about words or communication, it's about your identity. Deciding which language to speak to my daughter was stirring so many emotions in me because language is emotional.

The air-conditioning in Starbucks is chilly and I pull a shawl around my shoulders. The leather of the sofa feels cool beneath my legs as I ponder over our language complexities. I know Urdu is the right choice on paper, but in my heart, I hate having to choose. Martino can relate. He has chosen to speak German with Mina, but his heart wishes to sing all the songs and lullabies in Italian, the way he has grown up. We have gone back and forth multiple times deciding which language to speak to whom. Last month, we even attended a talk on raising multilingual kids organized by the American Club in Singapore. Meeting and hearing the stories of other bilingual and multilingual parents has been the only thing that has given me hope, even if I did leave the session with more questions than answers. How could we follow the 'One Person, One Language' model when we were clearly Two Parents with Two Languages? How could bilingual parents impart both of their languages to their children, while living as expats and away from grandparents and family members to lean on for language support?

I know one thing for sure. Raising multilingual kids is going to be one of the biggest challenges in my parenting journey. As with many other aspects of an international life, no one has prepared me for how to raise multilingual kids, so it is time to teach myself.

> **Choosing one language over another feels like I am denying part of who I am. Is it normal to feel this way? How does a bilingual parent 'let go' of one of their languages when it comes time to raise their own kids?**

LANGUAGES AS THE THREAD OF YOUR MOLA

Your multilingual background forms the thread of your mola. The languages that you speak in your family are the thread that helps to stitch your MOLA Family together. We use language to communicate, but when you are an international family living overseas and raising a family overseas, your communication varies greatly on the language(s) that you speak, the language(s) your partner speaks and the language(s) of the host country you live in.

Founder of Bilingual Potential, and author of the Bilingual Cake Book, Soile Pietikäinen is a sociologist specializing in bilingual family interaction. She explains the importance of teaching your child your native language: "Did you know that children's right to 'learn and use' the language(s) of their parents is enshrined in the most widely ratified human rights treaty of all time? The UN Convention on the Rights of the Child (UNCRC) is the foundation of the work of UNICEF. Article 30 of UNCRC spells out that wherever they live, children always have the right to their parent's language."

Soile further clarifies that, "Bilingual parenting is not about raising super-children. It is about living a happy and natural family life, where our love and care builds the foundation for our children's future. For many of us that involves more than one language because of who we love and where we live."

Speaking more than one language is not a rare phenomenon explains bilingual expert and author of several books on bilingualism, French professor Francois Grosjean: "It has been estimated that more than half the world's population is bilingual, that it lives with two or more languages. Bilingualism is found in all parts of the world, at all levels of society, in all age groups."

Nonetheless, there are many myths about raising a bilingual or multilingual child.

The prevailing discourse in many Western countries was that growing up with two or more languages 'confused' a child. People believed that a child raised bilingually or multilingually would learn to speak later than their monolingual peers and may or may not suffer speech impediments or delays. There were concerns about 'burdening' a child with more than two languages. In the UK, up till the 1970s, schools and teachers actively asked parents from immigrant backgrounds to speak English with their children, instead of their native languages – which reflected the lack of understanding and social stigma there was to speak a different language at home.

> "Bilingual parenting is not about raising super-children. It is about living a happy and natural family life, where our love and care builds the foundation for our children's future. For many of us that involves more than one language because of who we love and where we live."
> — Soile Pietikäinen.

BUSTING THE COMMON LANGUAGE MYTHS

Today, we know there is no research to support any of these claims. When children are learning two or more languages simultaneously it is quite common and in fact normal for them to mix their languages. "Mixing languages is not a sign of laziness in bilinguals," explains Francois Grosjean. Mixing languages is both inevitable and harmless. Francois further explains, "Mixing languages such as code-switching and borrowing is a very common behavior in bilinguals speaking to other bilinguals. It is a bit like having coffee with milk, instead of just straight black. Many expressions and words are better said in one or the other language; mixing permits to use the right one without a need to translate."

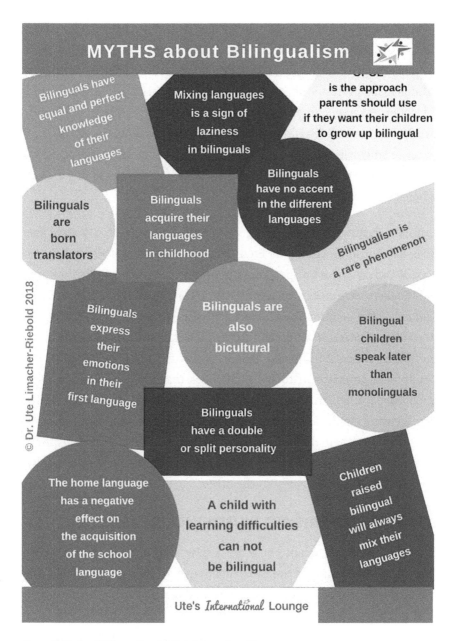

Figure 5: Myths of Bilingualism by Ute's International Lounge

Secondly, speaking two or more languages does not create any language delays. Children develop their language skills differently, whether they are monolingual or multilingual. Colin Baker, a researcher in childhood bilingualism presents his research findings in his book *The Care and Education of Young Bilinguals: An Introduction for Professionals* published in 2000 by stating, "Raising children bilingually is sometimes believed to cause language delay, though evidence does not support this position. Raising children bilingually neither increases nor reduces the chance of language disorder or delay."

Thirdly, learning to speak more than one language at a young age does not burden a child – as Fred Genesee, Professor of Psychology at McGill University, who specializes in second language acquisition and bilingualism research, explains in his 2015 paper *Myths About Early Childhood Bilingualism*. The article, which was published in the *Canadian Psychology Journal*, claims that bilingual acquisition is as natural as monolingual acquisition and that it is not an additional burden for children in comparison to the challenges that children learning one language face. On the contrary, it encourages them to practice skills like focusing, multitasking and weeding out unnecessary information. It also teaches them different ways to look at a problem, increases their cultural competence and increases their brain activity as they learn how to switch from one language to the other.

BENEFITS OF RAISING MULTILINGUAL KIDS

It is often said that when you learn a new language, you learn a new culture. I believe one of the best advantages of living a global life are the languages we come in contact with and learn to communicate in. I wanted to ensure that my children grew up not only amongst worlds, but also amongst languages. Language is also an interesting phenomenon because it is one of the most frequently mentioned challenges in international marriages, yet it is also an aspect of culture that parents strongly want to pass on to their cross-cultural children.

I wanted to ensure that my children grew up not only amongst worlds, but also amongst languages.

The substantial cognitive, social, personal, academic and professional benefits of multilingualism are well known. Multilingual children enjoy many benefits, some of them being:

- A keener awareness and sharper perception of language
- A better ear for listening and sharper memories
- The ability to parcel up and categorize meanings in different ways
- A greater cognitive flexibility, better problem-solving and high-order thinking skills
- The skill of being a more efficient communicator
- The ability to learn further languages more quickly and efficiently than their monolingual peers
- The ability to be simultaneously insiders and outsiders; to see their own culture from a new perspective not available to monoglots.

"A person who speaks multiple languages has a stereoscopic vision of the world from two or more perspectives, enabling them to be more flexible in their thinking, and learn to read more easily. Multilinguals, therefore, are not restricted to a single world-view, but also have a better understanding that other outlooks are possible," notes Vivian James Cook, the Emeritus Professor of Applied Linguistics at Newcastle University in the UK, who is renowned for his work on second language acquisition and second language teaching and has published more than 20 books and 100 papers in this field.

While the benefits of raising multilingual children are well researched and documented, many parents around the world still struggle to raise their kids with two or more languages. Choosing the right language framework and a consistent language strategy are key factors to success but also what most parents raising multilingual children often need help with.

"When it comes to raising children to speak more than one language, every family is unique. Many factors play a role in whether children pick up the languages they are exposed to and how fluent they become. A language setup that works brilliantly in one family may not suit another. There are also several right solutions – you just need to find the one that fits your family and circumstances. Don't expect your family's language journey to be the same as someone else's," advises Rita Rosenback. She further advises parents to:

"Weigh up your priorities and available time when choosing the language strategy for your family. When you have decided which languages you want your children to learn, you may find that your extended family and friends do not agree with you. Remember that this is your decision; your life as a family."

Dr. Ute Limacher-Riebold, a former lecturer in Linguistics at the Department of Romance Studies in Zurich, a researcher in multilingualism, and Language Consultant at Ute's International Lounge, agrees.

"Parents who keep their expectations realistic, whilst being open-minded, flexible and coherent at the same time, will find it easier to raise their children with more than one language. Knowing that there will always be one or two more dominant languages, that becoming bilingual requires time and constant dedication, that siblings may have different language preferences, and our children may have accents, code-switch regularly and even prefer not talking our home language for a while, will help parents set realistic goals," explains Ute.

DEFINITIONS AND EXAMPLES OF MULTILINGUAL FAMILIES

A multilingual family is one that is able to speak and understand several languages. Often the terms bilingual and multilingual are used interchangeably, since a bilingual person can communicate in two languages, while a multilingual person can communicate in two or more languages. Communication could be through speaking, listening, writing, reading or signing. You could be multilingual yourself, say, if you are fluent in Italian, Spanish and English, but perhaps you are raising your children bilingually with Italian and English.

There have been many books written on how to raise a bilingual child, but not so many on how to raise a multilingual child which often is the next step for parents who grew up bilingually themselves. It is this complexity in MOLA Families that is explored in this chapter. Raising multilingual kids when the parents are multilingual is tough and raising multilingual kids when the parents are monolingual is also tough. Both require patience and understanding.

LANGUAGE FRAMEWORKS AND FAMILY LANGUAGE GOALS

What are the different language frameworks out there? And how does a MOLA Family come up with a consistent language strategy and achieve their family language goals?

Below are some of the most popular ways to raise multilingual children. It is important to remember, though, that there can be pros and cons to each method.

LANGUAGE MODELS

1. One Person, One Language (OPOL)

This is the most popular method of raising multilingual kids. Each parent speaks to the child in one language consistently. The child is expected to respond in the language spoken to them and corrected if they respond in the 'wrong' language. For example, the mother speaks French and the father speaks English, so the child learns to speak French with his mother and English with his father. The main advantage of OPOL is that each parent speaking to the child is speaking their own mother tongue, so the child picks up the language to a native level and suffers no confusion with whom to speak which language. However, OPOL is criticized for not being a very flexible language method and may not necessarily work in families with more complicated language dynamics, where both parents don't have one native language but two or more. Also, many Third Culture Kids or Cross-Cultural Kids who grew up bilingually or multilingually, may in particular struggle with OPOL, because instead of imparting two or three of their languages, they can only impart one to their children.

2. Minority Language at Home (ML@H)

This is another popular method that many multilingual families adopt. In this framework, the minority language is spoken at home between the parents and the children, but out in the community and the school, the children speak the majority language. For example, a Bangladeshi family living in the UK might decide to speak Bengali at home with the kids, but the kids speak English (the community language) outside the home. The advantage of ML@H is that the whole family can speak together in one language and it increases the exposure the children are getting to their minority language. But one disadvantage that many families may feel, especially those with younger children, is that the same Bangladeshi kid may not have been exposed to the community language, so when they start school, they may be behind their peers.

3. The Time/Place Model (T&P)

This language method is based on contexts such as time and place. Families who decide to raise a multilingual child based on the T&P model, may decide that they switch languages depending on who they are with or where they are. For instance, the family members may decide to speak one language when their extended family visits, so that everyone can be included and understood. Or they may decide to speak different languages based on the days of the week, for example Sunday, Tuesday and Thursday are German days and Monday, Wednesday and Friday are Portuguese days. The advantage of this method is that the families get used to speaking and switching between languages and the children make the important connection between language and context and learn which language to speak to with whom and when. However, this method risks inconsistency and thus confusion (especially with kids under five who may not understand the rules) and could lead to them developing preferred languages to communicate in.

4. Mixing languages or 'code-switching'

Many multilingual parents find it hard to choose only one language to speak consistently with their kids. They might have grown up with several different languages themselves and hence like to sing to their children in Hindi, but speak in English, or scold them in Punjabi. Such families mix their languages and switch from speaking one language to the next, which is referred to as 'code-switching.'

This particular form of multilingualism is common in countries that have an official second language (such as Canada) or many languages (South Africa has 11 official languages, while Switzerland and Singapore have four official languages each). And in countries like India and Pakistan boasting a large number of indigenous and regional languages combined with a complex history of more than 200 years of British colonialism, it has led to English becoming part of their multilingual psyche as well. The advantages are that you don't need a plan, you speak as comes naturally to you. But the disadvantage is that children may start to favor one language over another, so they may be proficient in one, and fall behind in the other language.

5. Two Parents, Two Languages (2P, 2L)

In this approach, parents are bilingual themselves and use both languages in their interaction with the kids. The language choice depends on several factors. Schoolwork may be done in the language used at school, while movies and books are seen/read in their original languages. The bilingual parents show their kids how to switch languages which is the norm for their family. The advantage is that bilingual parents do not need to suppress one of their native languages in favor of another; they can express them fully in both of their languages. The disadvantage of this method is that it can be hard to motivate a child to speak two languages with each parent and not settle on just speaking one.

Language strategy and language goals

It is important for each multilingual family to clearly outline what their specific family language strategy and family language goals are.

"Whatever language strategy you choose, make sure that your partner, your children's siblings, extended family, teachers, friends etc., your *village*, is on board: you need a village to raise a multilingual child," advises Ute Limacher-Riebold.

The clearer the family language goals are, the higher the chance of success. For example, if a Chinese mother is speaking in Mandarin to her children, what is her overall language goal? Is it that:

- Her children can understand Mandarin (demonstrate passive knowledge of the language).
- Her children can speak and respond in fluent Mandarin (demonstrate active knowledge of the language).
- Her children can read in Mandarin (demonstrate literacy in the language).
- Her children can write in Mandarin (demonstrate literacy in the language).

"Whatever language strategy you choose, make sure that your partner, your children's siblings, extended family, teachers, friends etc., your village, is on board: you need a village to raise a multilingual child."

— Ute Limacher-Riebold.

For example, my language goal is that my children can speak and understand fluent Urdu. I read to them in Urdu too, but am not focusing on teaching them how to write in Urdu. Writing in Urdu is not one of my language goals for them (yet), as they are unlikely to need to write to anyone in Urdu.

THE CHALLENGES AND OPPORTUNITIES OF A MULTILINGUAL FAMILY – OUR EXPERTS ADVISE

Ask a multilingual family what their challenges are in raising multilingual kids and you will hear a whole range of concerns and issues. I collected data from hundreds of international families through *The Mobile Family Survey* in 2018, through which participants shared their experiences from around the world. I chose a few examples of the challenges faced by multilingual families and asked my team of three language experts to offer some advice and solutions.

MEET THE MOLA FAMILIES

Russian Mother and Australian Father Raise Multilingual Kids in Dubai

Alena is from Russia, while her husband is from Australia. Alena has lived in both Moscow and Perth, but currently lives in Dubai with her husband and two young sons who are five and three years old. Her kids attend a multilingual preschool in Dubai, where they learn in English, Arabic and French. Alena explains that as a cross-cultural couple raising their children abroad, language is her main concern.

"Supporting my mother tongue with my children is difficult as they have no exposure to Russian socially, it is only spoken by me.

It's been a constant struggle for me to keep the Russian language alive in our family. Ever since the children started talking, they chose English as their main language for expressing themselves even though I only spoke Russian to them. To date, I am losing this battle. I inevitably switched to English when speaking to them for ease of day-to-day communication. Now if that wasn't bad enough, their Russian grandmother visiting twice a year is eating me alive for not speaking Russian with my kids, as it's apparently so easy because I'm a native speaker, right?" asks Alena.

o o o

Q: WHAT STEPS CAN ALENA TAKE TO RE-ENFORCE HER NATIVE LANGUAGE OF RUSSIAN WITH HER CHILDREN?

A: Expert Rita Rosenback has some advice for Alena and her multilingual family:

Dear Alena,

You have not lost the battle. You are going through a challenging phase of your family's Russian language journey, but you can reach your goal. Your children did not reject Russian: English just happened to be easier. Children are very pragmatic. When they want to communicate, they do so in a way they find easiest.

It is hard to be the only person speaking a language with a child. Life is hectic. It is understandable that you switched to English to get your message across. Don't blame yourself. Think positively about what you have already achieved. Your children have a foundation in Russian and can understand a lot of what is said. Build on this.

Reaffirm your language priorities: what would happen if your kids grew up not speaking Russian? When you know in your heart that you strongly want them to speak Russian, it is easier to introduce and maintain routines to support this.

Create fun situations where your children will want and need to use Russian. Use songs, rhymes and simple games. Introduce a toy (e.g. hand puppet) which understands and speaks only Russian. Create a dedicated space in your home where everything is Russian: pictures, books, toys, music, ornaments, home furnishings and so on. When you are in this space, only use Russian. Gradually use more Russian around the home.

Grandmother's visits should be something to look forward to! Set the expectations: emphasize the importance of her support for Russian; ask for her help. Actively ignore any negative comments – you know best.

You can do this!
Rita

Venezuelan-American Parents Raise Teenage TCKs in Germany

Flor is from Venezuela, but also holds US citizenship. Her husband was born in the United States, but also has Venezuelan nationality. Flor's first language is Spanish, but she also speaks English and German and is learning French. Her husband is bilingual in English and Spanish and is learning German. Flor and her husband are raising three TCK teenagers (aged 12, 13 and 14), all born in Texas, but currently living in Germany. Flor speaks Spanish with her kids, but her husband speaks English with the kids. The children's preferred language is English.

"For us, the most difficult part of this journey so far has been to keep the Spanish language 'alive.' Even though, I always speak to the kids in my native language and I raise them with a strong Venezuelan influence, they refuse to speak it. They understand and communicate with family members who don't speak English or German, however it isn't their language of choice and they pronounce it with a very heavy accent. It becomes a problem because sometimes the children don't want to have long conversations with grandparents and relatives because of the language. They are somehow too lazy to put together sentences in Spanish. What do we do? I promote reading and listening to music in Spanish, traveling to Spain and Venezuela frequently and video calls with relatives every Sunday. Also, my boys have already started Spanish at school and their language skills have improved. My daughter will start next year," explains Flor.

o o o

Q: HOW CAN FLOR MOTIVATE HER TEENAGERS TO SPEAK SPANISH, WHEN THEIR PREFERRED LANGUAGES ARE ENGLISH AND GERMAN?

A: **Expert Ute Limacher-Riebold has some advice for Flor and her multilingual family:**

Dear Flor,

Your story presents some common issues that many multilingual families encounter. Your children prefer speaking English and have a "heavy accent", although you speak Spanish with them and teach them Spanish at home. Your children were schooled in English first and now in German, therefore these are their most important and dominant languages. Many parents underestimate the impact of the school language on their children and are surprised that it becomes their preferred and most dominant one.

Your children probably don't want "to have long conversations in Spanish with grandparents and relatives" because they struggle finding the right words, and because someone pointed out their lack of fluency. This leads to a lack of confidence that should be addressed: extended families, caregivers, teachers need to collaborate in supporting these children with their home language. In this particular case: an accent free and native fluent proficiency in Venezuelan Spanish seems to be an unrealistic goal.

Although you mention that they visit Spain and Venezuela regularly, the Spanish in these two countries differs slightly and can unintentionally contribute to the children's overall confusion and lack of confidence. Full immersion usually boosts children's language skills, especially if they are involved in activities with peers, as they are crucial for teenagers: driven by the general need to fit in, they learn the slang, discover what music, movies, shows are cool, pick up new vocabulary naturally and gain confidence.

The "laziness to speak Spanish" that you describe is probably happening mainly in family settings, as all family members also speak English and the children simply use the most economical way to communicate by choosing the language everyone understands and is most comfortable with: English.

Your family is currently using the OPOL (One Person, One Language) and ML/@H (Minority Language at Home) strategies. I would suggest adding the T&P (Time and Place) one, by introducing a Spanish-only day, preferably on weekends, when the whole family is more relaxed.

Having your husband join them will have a considerable impact on the children, as he will send the message that Spanish is a valuable language: that day they can listen to Spanish songs, eat Spanish meals, read Spanish books, switch the language of their devices to Spanish etc. and enjoy speaking the language.

Despite your older children having started Spanish lessons at school recently, they seem to be motivated as their Spanish skills are improving. It is important to keep this momentum going and foster their motivation by providing them input on topics they are interested in.

The fact that, in opposition to her older siblings, your youngest was mainly schooled in German, means that all your children have different language preferences and proficiencies, which is very common in multilingual families.

Best,
Ute.

A Swedish/Thai ATCK Mother and a British Father Raise Multilingual Kids in Dubai

Mireille grew up as a Third Culture Kid (TCK) with her parents hailing from Sweden and Thailand. She thus holds both Swedish and Thai nationalities. She lists Swedish, English, Swahili and Thai as her native languages. She has lived in Thailand, Indonesia, Sweden, UK, USA, Libya, Kenya, Tanzania and the UAE. Her husband is from the UK and holds British and Irish citizenship. His native language is English. As a couple, they have lived in the UK and the UAE. Their first child was born in 2010 in Dubai where they currently live, so their eight-year-old child has not experienced any international moves. Mireille finds that as a multilingual ATCK raised with many languages, raising her own multilingual family is proving to be a challenge. Her husband does not speak Swedish, Swahili or Thai, so English becomes the default language in her home.

"As a TCK myself raised in a multilingual household, with each of my parents' mother tongues being different from each other, our third language was English. My child is now studying Arabic and Mandarin in school, but with all of us speaking English fluently, it is difficult to keep up and help teach Swedish – especially to my own child. Third Culture Kids are normally good with languages, but never a master in one," says Mireille.

o o o

Q: WHAT STEPS CAN MIREILLE TAKE TO PASS ON HER NATIVE TONGUE OF SWEDISH TO HER CHILD? AND IS A MULTILINGUAL ADULT THIRD CULTURE KID (ATCK) LIKE MIREILLE FORCED TO CHOOSE ONLY ONE NATIVE LANGUAGE TO TEACH HER CHILD AND LOSE THE OTHER LANGUAGES SHE GREW UP WITH?

A: Expert Soile Pietikäinen has some advice for Mireille and ATCKs like her on letting a language go:

Dear Mireille,

Thank you for this wonderful question. For native bilinguals the passage from being a bilingual child to a bilingual parent involves letting go. There is a process of grief in coming to terms with the fact that our multiple languages are not our child's languages, no matter how much joy they bring to us.

We need to focus on the languages our child needs for their own unique life. It sounds to me that for your child these languages would be English, and if you plan to stay longer in the UAE, standard modern Arabic. It is important for children to become independent members of a society they grow up in. That means understanding the society in its own language.

It sounds like in Swedish, your family has experienced the very common language loss that happens when one parent speaks a minority language at home. My question is, does your child really need Swedish? This may be a surprising point of view. Let's take it step by step.

Multilingual family life is often talked about in the short term, focusing on parents and children during the first years of a child's life. But life is long and families are extended. This needs to be taken into account when a native multilingual parent is making hard choices about which one of their languages to use for the parenting relationship with their children.

I will share some generic guidance on how a multilingual parent can choose which language to parent in. This applies to all multilingual parents. This can also help you decide whether you need to invest in Swedish in your family or not.

There are three main factors:

1. **Linguistic competence and the long-term needs of parenting:** We need to choose to parent in a language in which we know we will be comfortable and skilled to handle the demands of the hardest emotional and intellectual challenges at any age. It needs to be a language in which we react at lightning speed to warn our young child of danger, but also the language in

which we can discuss world news and adult relationships with our 18-year-old. Do not be tempted to start parenting in your weaker language unless that is the native language of your partner. You will either have to change the language of your parent-child bond or settle for low quality conversations. Prevent these two things from happening.

2. **Emotional attachment:** Many bilingual parents call this the language of their heart. For parenting we need to choose a language in which we can live a rich family life in the privacy of our homes. This could be one of the languages you associate with parental love in your childhood home or the native language of your partner. The languages of a multilingual person are differentiated by use. We may appear near native speakers or at least very advanced users of a particular language in one context but be completely at a loss for words in another context. This is why native bilinguals and multilinguals are not particularly good translators.

3. **Family relationships:** Our children need a sense of family belonging that goes beyond the home they share with their parents. Globally mobile children really need this connection, as they will never truly belong to any one society and that is tough. Their two extended families are their cultural anchor. Children need good relationships with grandparents. In a multilingual family this means choosing to parent in a language that both of our parents speak well. When you meet your parents and siblings, what is the language you use so that everyone can share the same story, joke or conversation? That is the language in which your child can belong in your family.

For all multilingual parents:

Did all three criteria bring you to the same language? Good, easy choice.

Did different criteria point to different languages? Prioritize in order of this list.

Mireille, you could start by listening to your child's thoughts and feelings about the Swedish language. Talk about it many times over several weeks. Just ask open questions and accept what your child says, asking further questions to extend the conversation.

See if Swedish comes up under any of the three criteria above. Maybe it does and maybe you discover that your child would really like to speak Swedish. If so, in a situation where an eight-year-old has largely stopped speaking a language, a speech activation strategy would require an analysis of your child's real-life language use.

However, maybe Swedish did not come up in your three-step analysis. That is okay. Now you know that both of you and your child can relax about Swedish and radically lower your expectations. A few Swedish expressions can be a joy.

You can move on to think about your child's unique international life. What is the second language that your child needs the most for their own living environment and their meaningful relationships?

Best,
Soile.

A Latvian Mother and a Dutch Father Raise a Multilingual Kid in the Netherlands

Kristine was born in Turkmenistan and holds Latvian and Dutch nationalities. She lists Latvian as her native language, but she also speaks Russian, English and Dutch. Her husband is from the Netherlands and his native language is Dutch, while he also speaks English, German and French. Together, they live in the Netherlands, where their first child was born in 2016. Kristine's biggest challenge when it comes to raising her 19-month-old son is around the question of exposure to a language.

"Teaching a minority language is not easy. My son loves books and it has been easy to find them in Latvian. But making sure that he hears Latvian from other people has been the biggest challenge. I know that teaching Latvian to my son will become a bigger challenge as he gets older," says Kristine.

o o o

Q: CAN A CHILD LEARN A MINORITY LANGUAGE IF HE HEARS IT FROM ONE PERSON ONLY? WHAT OTHER STEPS CAN KRISTINE TAKE TO INCREASE HIS EXPOSURE TO HIS MINORITY LANGUAGE OF LATVIAN?

A: **Expert Soile Pietikäinen has some advice for Kristine on language exposure:**

Dear Kristine,

I have some good news for you. Your success in bilingual parenting does not depend on exposure. There are only two things that truly matter in bilingual parenting: great conversations and reading books. You are already doing great on reading books. The quality of conversation depends on you.

The best thing you can do is to learn superb conversation strategies and help your child to develop conversational turn-taking skills. Have a lot of conversations where you speak Latvian and your child responds in baby language. Make these exchanges as long as feels natural.

It would be ideal if Latvian were developing faster than Dutch for several years. To achieve this, it is crucial to turn the sounds your child is making into real words in Latvian. Once new words are appearing every day you can start establishing two-way conversations in Latvian. Start from shifting the focus from your speech to the child's speech. Create eye contact. Listen to your son's attempts to say words and react to them. Communicate positive interest. Say to your child the word you think he meant and encourage him to say it again with you.

At the age of 18-24 months, you can expect to see vocabulary growth in both languages, paving the way for the first two-word sentences emerging towards the second birthday.

It is more than possible to raise children with two native languages with just one parent using a language with them. Bilingual parenting success happens at home.

Best,
Soile.

American Parents Raise Bilingual Kids in Sweden

Lisa and her husband are both Americans, whose first language is English. Lisa lists both Spanish and Swedish as the languages she and her husband have acquired en route. They currently live in Sweden, where they are raising their two children aged seven and five bilingually with Swedish and English. Their son was only nine months old when they made the move from the US to Sweden and their daughter was born in Sweden. In recent years, their whole family has received Swedish citizenship, making them dual American/Swedish citizens. As parents whose kids are schooled in a language different than their home language, Lisa explains that her biggest challenge in raising their bilingual kids is helping them navigate the outside world.

"Language continues to be a struggle within my home. We speak English exclusively at home, but our children are bilingual and navigate the outside world easily. The parents? Not so easily, because we both work in English and learning another language has been difficult. The biggest challenge is when I am speaking to my kids' school teachers. I can speak everyday Swedish, which means I can understand about 65% of what the teachers are telling me, while they think I'm comprehending everything just fine," explains Lisa.

o o o

Q: HOW CAN PARENTS LIKE LISA BEST SUPPORT THEIR CHILDREN'S BILINGUAL/MULTILINGUAL EDUCATION IN A LANGUAGE THAT IS DIFFERENT FROM THEIR HOME LANGUAGE?

A: Expert Ute Limacher-Riebold has some advice for Lisa whose children are schooled in a language different than their home language:

Dear Lisa,

You mention that you find it difficult to communicate in the local language of Swedish in a specific context. This is a very common problem among international families, especially when working in an environment where the local language is not used on a daily basis or to a very limited extent.

I advise parents like you whose children are schooled in another language than their home language, to learn how to speak with the teachers - communication in Swedish is very different from English and if one is not that fluent yet, it is difficult to avoid misunderstandings, like the one you mention.

As parents, you can avoid this kind of misunderstandings or frustration by preparing for meetings like the one you mention, with specific questions and goals in mind. Your questions can help the teachers formulate the information in a more comprehensive way. It can be specific questions about the curriculum, the vocabulary they used at school, what is expected from the children and their parents. It is also advisable to be very clear of your own expectations as well.

Parents whose children are schooled in another language ought to learn not only the other language, but also understand how to function in everyday situations, perhaps with the help of an intercultural communication trainer.

This is important because your multilingual children need your support throughout their time at school. They learn to read, write, do math, science etc. in their school language. In order to make sure they fully understand the topics and are able to talk about them in your home language, you need to help them make a bridge between the school language and the home language.

Raising a bi- or multilingual child means so much more than fostering the language; it means to transmit the culture, its values, norms and beliefs and the understanding of "how things are done."

Best,
Ute.

All the MOLA Families acknowledged that their multilingual lifestyle brought forth many opportunities as well. Raising children with different languages helped in their development and progress at school. It made it easier for them to learn a foreign language at school. It made them open and more tolerant of different linguistic backgrounds and it increased their understanding and knowledge of the world around them.

A Senegalese/French Mother and a Mauritian/French Father Raise Multilingual Kids in Dubai

Mariama comes from Senegal and holds both Senegalese and French nationalities. She is a native speaker of French and Wolof and learned to speak English later in life. Her partner comes from France, holds both French and Mauritian nationalities and is fluent in French and English. Together they have lived in France, South Korea and the UAE. Their four-year-old was born in France and their three-year-old in South Korea, while they currently live in Dubai. For Mariama, one of the best aspects of their global lives is the communication advantages her children enjoy, as a result of exposure to many languages.

"I am so happy that both my kids can switch from English to French and can even have some sentences in Wolof (our Senegalese language). I am so happy when my son comes back to me in the playground to tell me he cannot borrow the new neighbor's bike because she speaks Arabic and he doesn't know yet how to borrow a bike in Arabic but that he will learn it soon. And with all the already available languages, he is keen on learning Spanish too. Welcome to the global world!" exclaims Mariama.

Rita Rosenback agrees there are many joys in raising children to speak more than one language and summarizes the 7C's that parents like Mariama need, in order to navigate their family's multilingual journey:

1. **Communication.** Discuss which languages you want your children to learn, and how fluently. Define and agree your goals. Be realistic with your own time.

2. **Confidence.** You can do this. When in doubt speak with other parents, but don't assume that their solutions suit you. Contact an expert coach when you need help with your family's language strategy.

3. **Commitment.** Commit to your goals and plan, and to supporting each other. However, revisit your plan and change it if you do not see the results you want.

4. **Consistency.** If you are the only person speaking a language with your child and have limited time to interact in it, the importance of being consistent in using the language increases. Don't set yourself up for disappointment by trying to achieve more than what is possible. Ask for help and look for other solutions.

5. **Creativity.** Creative actions may be needed to arrange enough language exposure for your child. Could you start a playgroup in a specific language, or hire a student to spend time with your kids?

6. **Culture.** Languages are intrinsically intertwined with culture. Teach your kids about the cultures of the languages they are learning. Travel whenever you can.

7. **Celebration.** Give yourself and each other a pat on the back for any progress made. Once they are grown up, your kids will be deeply thankful for your efforts.

YOUR MOLA TOOLBOX: O IS FOR ORDER

As I carried a tray full of snacks up to Mina's room, I paused at her front door. It was then that I heard my five-year-old say out loud to her friend who was over for a playdate after school,

"Your papa doesn't speak a different language than your mama? They both speak the same language to you?" she asked with a puzzled look on her face.

Her friend nodded.

"That's so weird!" exclaimed Mina.

I wanted to laugh and cry tears of joy at the same time. Clearly, my daughter had grown up thinking a multilingual family like ours was the norm, so she now found it strange when her friend revealed that both her parents spoke the same language.

How had we reached this point? Through a lot of hard work, tears and a few rebellions as well. What I learned though is that when it comes to raising a multilingual family, order is key. Therefore, in my framework of a MOLA Family, O stands for Order. The second rule of creating a MOLA Family is to bring order into your family lives by having a clearly defined language method, strategy and goals.

The first thing you need to do is to find a strategy that will work best for you and your family. It could be OPOL, it could be ML@H or it could be something else. Once you decide what suits your family best, given the number of languages you speak, where you live, schooling options, each parent's fluency in the language they hope to impart and so on, the important thing is to be consistent. If you have no order and no structure, your multilingual goals will be harder to achieve. Remember, different strategies will work for different families.

HOW DID I CREATE ORDER IN MY MULTILINGUAL FAMILY?

We started off with practicing OPOL – One Person, One Language. Martino and I each chose one native language to speak to with the kids. He chose German. I chose Urdu. We continued to speak to each other in predominantly English, with German and Urdu thrown in for good measure, and the kids started speaking in English with each other too while living in Dubai. We actively decided that Italian would be spoken to them by their Italian grandfather but accepted that since he does not live near us and the kids do not see him every day, they would at best gain a passive knowledge of Italian.

Sometimes when the kids fought, they would fight in German (Mina) and Urdu (Mikail) but reach a truce in English. It was similar for the parents. When we fought, Martino swore in Italian, and I went into a tirade in Urdu, before we made up in English. Our languages became cues for the emotions we were feeling as well.

Our language goals for our children were thus:

- German: fluency in speaking, understanding, reading and writing.
- Urdu: fluency in speaking, understanding and reading (writing was a goal we tackled later and indirectly through Arabic, but not directly).
- English: fluency in speaking, understanding, reading and writing.
- Italian: passive knowledge only, being able to understand the language.
- Mandarin: after our move from Singapore to Dubai, when Mina was two and a half years old we let Mandarin go reluctantly. We didn't have the means or resources for her to continue learning this language after the move.
- Arabic: we were happy with anything our children learned in Arabic, but our main goal was to use Arabic taught at school to help introduce a new alphabet and script to the kids, which is similar to Urdu. Mina has started writing in Arabic, which means she can also write in Urdu.

Did everything work smoothly for us?

No, of course not.

We followed strict OPOL for four years, but I started to realize OPOL was not working for me and was making me miserable as a multilingual parent. I felt stressed trying to speak 100% Urdu all the time with my kids. And then I realized why. No one in Pakistan – especially in the social circle that I come from – speaks 100% in Urdu. The reality is that we code-switch a lot between English, Urdu and for many families also between regional languages like Sindhi or Punjabi. It is difficult for multilingual societies to stay consistent in one language. Trying to force myself and denying the natural way in which I talked, was why I was feeling miserable.

I also realized that I did not want to teach my children some antiquated form of a language that no one really spoke in reality. Language is about understanding and being able to communicate. For me, it meant redefining my language goals to ditch teaching my kids some perfect or ideal state of a language and rather focus on teaching them a realistic, useable communication toolbox. Mina and Mikail will be expected to code-switch in Pakistan, so I had to sew this linguistic reality into our MOLA Family.

ONE PERSON, ONE LANGUAGE (OPOL) OR CODE-SWITCHING?

I continued speaking in Urdu with both kids, but when I felt like inserting an English word or phrase, I would insert it right in. Most people would probably tell me to "wait a minute you are not being consistent", but for me code-switching WAS being consistent. And I realized that I could not compare a language like Urdu or Hindi to Spanish or Greek. All these languages had developed differently. In Pakistan, our colonial background and legacy meant that many English words were incorporated and accepted into the Urdu language. When my father one day complained he was suffering from "high blood pressure" I asked him why he didn't say that in Urdu, like the rest of his sentence. We both laughed as we wracked our brains to think of how to translate "high blood pressure" in Urdu. Dictionaries were brought out and Google Translate was consulted. Even my grandparents who spoke fluent Urdu would have used "high blood pressure" in their sentence instead of *"bulund fashar-e khoon"* in Urdu, which sounds weird and antiquated to our ears since almost no one would use it nowadays.

I also started observing my parents-in-law, who would code-switch constantly between Italian and German. My German mother-in-law would start talking about her work at the Italian Consulate in Germany, in German, but then switch over to Italian when relating what a colleague said, or what was in the email she received. My Italian father-in-law, who worked for a German car company, would start talking about his day in Italian, but when it came to the complex automobile technology or work processes, he automatically would switch to German.

Francois Grosjean explains code-switching as a normal occurrence between bilinguals: "In a bilingual mode, once a base language has been chosen, bilinguals can bring in the other language in various ways. One of these ways is to code-switch, this is to shift completely to the other language for a word, a phrase, a sentence. The other way is to borrow a word or short expression from that language and to adapt it morphologically (and often phonologically) into the base language. Thus, unlike code-switching, which is the juxtaposition of two languages, borrowing is the integration of one language into another."

I decided that in our MOLA Family, code-switching and borrowing was often the norm. So, we became a bit more flexible in our language approach. My husband still speaks to the kids in German and reads to them exclusively in German, but if he feels like singing to them in Italian at bedtime or in the car during long road trips, he does. I continue speaking to the kids in Urdu, but if I cannot remember how to say something in Urdu, I simply use the English word for it, instead of trying to be consistent just for the sake of being consistent. We still follow this order, but because it allows both of us more room to parent naturally, it feels like a better fit for our particular family.

Rita Rosenback has the following advice: "Be as consistent as you can, but also don't let the striving for consistency become something so rigid that it takes away the joy from speaking your language or, even worse, creates a communication barrier. Language is all about making connections and creating bonds through communication. If the opposite happens, then it is time to review how the languages are used in the family. With this, I am not saying at all that you should not try to steer your child to use the right language, for example by repeating in your language what your child just said to you in the 'other' language, and thus creating a natural bridge back to the preferred one. It is about finding the right balance between the two extremes."

WHY ORDER CAN HELP YOUR MOLA FAMILY

Your languages are the thread that stitches your MOLA Family together. If your children don't speak your language, they won't feel connected to your culture – it will be like a loose piece of cloth that is just hanging there, but not incorporated into the overall design of your mola.

In order to incorporate all the different elements of your multilingual family, it is imperative to have some order. Order does not mean you need to be rigid or set in stone; on the contrary, order means having a plan and introducing changes to the plan if you feel something is not working. Many multilingual families go through changes all the time. A new sibling can change the family's language dynamics, as can an international move.

The more ambitious your family language goals are, the more order will help. Order is also important to help deal with the inevitable rebellions that will come your way. Children will always choose the path of least resistance, and as parents it is important to not only expect this eventuality but also prepare for it.

Your languages are the thread that stitches your MOLA Family together. If your children don't speak your language, they won't feel connected to your culture – it will be like a loose piece of cloth just hanging there, but not incorporated into the overall design of your mola.

When Mina was three years old, we experienced our first major rebellion. It was around this time that she started attending nursery in Dubai and figured out that her Mama and Papa can both speak English, so why should she speak to us in Urdu and German respectively?

She started rebelling. Instead of calling Martino, Papa, she started calling him Daddy and speaking to him in English. He stayed strong and refused to answer or talk in English. It felt like history was repeating itself.

When Martino was four years old, he too had rebelled. As a young child growing up in Germany, he had questioned why he needed to speak in Italian with his Italian father, when he knew his father also spoke fluent German? My Italian father-in-law, Salvatore, had remained firm and insisted, "Either you speak Italian with me, or you don't speak to me at all."

It might sound harsh, but it worked. Martino today speaks fluent Italian and can read and write in Italian too. People are constantly amazed at his Italian, given the fact he has never lived in Italy.

This story also highlights two important principles in raising multilingual children:

1. As a parent, you need to create a need for your child to speak your language. My father-in-law did just that by reinforcing that if Martino wanted to talk to him, it had to be in Italian.

2. "Children become bilingual by speaking the language, not by hearing a parent speak it," explains Soile. As a parent, you need to decide whether you expect your child to have a passive or active knowledge of your language. My father-in-law was clear in his language goal for Martino. Unlike many other Italian immigrants to Germany, he was not happy if his son understood Italian (passive knowledge) but couldn't speak Italian (active knowledge). Many immigrant parents continue to speak their native language to their child, so the child understands everything they say, but if they accept answers from their child in a different language (often the majority language), then the child never learns how to form a sentence or speak the language actively. This is what Martino tried; he tested if his father would accept answers from him in German, but he didn't. The message was clear: only Italian would be accepted in their father and son relationship. To create a bilingual child, you must focus on active knowledge by insisting the child speaks to you in your language.

When faced with his own daughter's rebellion, Martino tried a similar tactic. He told Mina, "Either you speak to me in German, or you don't speak to me at all."

I winced. It sounded incredibly harsh, but it was important to reinforce the language order we had decided on. And it was important to create a need for Mina to be able to speak in German and to insist on her actively speaking in this language. It took Martino almost two years of consistent hard work, but he succeeded. Today Mina and Mikail both take it for granted that they speak with their papa in German.

THE FIVE RULES FOR MULTILINGUAL FAMILIES

1. TAKE ADVANTAGE OF THE WINDOWS OF LEARNING IN A CHILD DEVELOPMENT JOURNEY

There are times in early childhood where the brain is better equipped to receive new languages. Experts agree, the first window of opportunity is from birth to nine months old. The second window of opportunity is from four to seven years old. And the third window of opportunity is from eight to adult. Once you as a parent have determined which window your child is in, you are able to decide how best to support them in the learning and development phase they are in. In her book *Raising Multilingual Children* Tracey Tokuhama-Espinosa argues that all three windows of opportunity provide for the possibility of proficient language acquisition but that, "children who learn their languages in the first window of opportunity (zero to nine months old) are always proficient bilinguals if their parents are consistent in the language strategy they use."

2. BE CONSISTENT IN WHICHEVER FRAMEWORK YOU CHOOSE

Language acquisition is best approached and tackled by adopting a consistent approach. Once you decide on your language strategy and goals, stick to them. Once you as a parent decide which language to speak to your child, stick to it. However, consistency does not mean that you continue doing something, even if you feel it's not working. Do not make adjustments or changes in strategy randomly, but after some thinking, evaluation, and soul searching. Rita explains why consistency is vital: "My opinion about the importance of consistency is based on the finding that children from families where parents are consistent in their language use are more likely to become active speakers of both (or all) of the languages of the family. Another reason I am an advocate for consistency is that it creates a habit. When speaking a certain language becomes a routine in a family, the language has more staying power than if it is used in a more random manner."

Soile agrees and explains that "for globally mobile families the risk is several underdeveloped languages, which might have serious consequences for social, emotional and linguistic development. Globally mobile families need to prevent this from happening by keeping the family language environment consistent and investing in at least one family language developing to a native standard. In a globally mobile life, your family is the one stable thing. Invest in it." In our highly mobile family for instance we agree to stay consistent in our home languages, no matter which country we live in: Martino will stay consistent in speaking German with the kids and I will stay consistent in speaking Urdu with the kids and code-switching in English when necessary. This helps to provide the kids with stability and continuity whether we live in Dubai or Paris.

3. PERSEVERANCE PAYS OFF

Many parents who are on the right track give up too soon. Be prepared that different amounts of perseverance will be required for different cases, but it will pay off. Many parents give up at the first sign of setbacks, delays or rebellions, even though these are normal parts of the process of language learning. Perseverance also requires both parents to be on the same page and to support each other in their interaction with their children. There is no such thing as smooth sailing when you're raising multilingual kids. To help our family persevere, we aim to have family dinners together every night. The aim is to sit down at the same table to persevere in our family communication style: kids speak to Martino in German and ask him for water in German, while the kids ask me for more bread but in Urdu. English is also used at our table but only between parent to parent or sibling to sibling. Thus, if Mikail would like more cucumber on his plate, he can either ask Martino in German, me in Urdu or Mina in English.

4. CREATE A NEED TO SPEAK THE LANGUAGE

This is probably the most important rule for any multilingual family. Unless the parents create a need to speak the language, children will develop only a passive knowledge of that language; they will understand what is being said, but won't demonstrate an active knowledge, meaning they won't be able to speak in the language themselves. Passive knowledge is easier to learn, while active knowledge can only happen if the parents create a need to speak the language. I have heard of some great techniques used by parents to do this, such as bringing home a pet but insisting their new puppy only understands the minority language, forcing the kids to start speaking in it. A Japanese-American friend living in the US would ask her mother living in Japan to send a big box of Japanese books, puzzles, music or toys to create an interest in her kids to learn Japanese. If you don't create a need to speak a particular language, your children will see no benefit in learning to speak in it.

5. RAISING MULTILINGUAL CHILDREN IS NOT A COMPETITIVE SPORT

Be careful in comparing progress with other multilingual children, as each situation and each MOLA Family is different with a unique constellation of elements. While it is useful to listen to stories of other multilingual families to help get inspired and feel supported, it can be difficult to compare individual circumstances and results. Each child develops or learns at his or her own pace. Each sibling dynamic is different. You will see enough variations in experience even in your own family.

CHAPTER SUMMARY

1. Your multilingual background is the thread of your MOLA Family. Just as the languages you speak help you to communicate, they are the thread that stitches your mola together and 'joins the dots.'

2. Multilingual kids do not suffer any additional burdens, speech delays or problems. The benefits of multilingualism are well researched and documented.

3. Some of the challenges faced by multilingual parents include: staying consistent; insisting on the child replying in the parents' native tongue; increasing exposure to a language; creating a need to speak the language and to raise multilingual kids even if the parents are monolingual. But the best opportunities enjoyed by multilingual families include increased cultural competence and understanding and tolerance of the world around them.

4. In your MOLA toolbox, O stands for order. In creating a MOLA Family, it is important for multilingual families to bring order by choosing a language model, strategy and goals. Order helps MOLA Families to stay focused and prepares them for dealing with rebellions.

5. To bring order to your multilingual family, it is important to take advantage of the early windows of language acquisition, to be consistent in whichever language framework you choose, persevere even in the face of setbacks or rebellions, create a need to speak a language, and to remember each MOLA Family is different.

ACTIVITY: CREATE YOUR FAMILY LANGUAGE PROFILE

It is time for you, the parent, to create your own family language profile. In order to do so please sit down with a piece of paper and first answer the following questions:

General/background:

- What is/are your native language or languages?
- What language(s) do you speak to your child or children in?
- What is/are your partner's native language or languages?
- Which country or countries were your children born in?
- What language(s) does your partner speak to your child or children in?
- What language(s) do you communicate in with your partner?
- What language(s) do your children communicate in as siblings?
- What language(s) do the children's nanny/caregiver speak to them in (if applicable)?
- Which country do you currently live in?
- Which country or countries have you raised your children in?
- How old are your children?
- How old were your children at the time of each international move?
- What is/are the dominant language(s) of the child at school?
- Does each child receive instruction in another language in addition to the dominant language?
- What is/are the community language(s)?

Family language strategy:

- What family language strategy do you follow? (OPOL, ML@H, T&P, and so on.)
- Is this working well for you?
- How long have you been following this strategy?
- Have you remained consistent with following this strategy?
- What setbacks have you faced? How did you deal with them?

Family language goals:

Do you want your child(ren) to be able to:

- Speak your native language fluently?
- Speak your partner's native language fluently?
- Speak well enough to visit and understand relatives in country X?
- Speak well enough to be able to play with other kids their age?
- Read in both their first, second and third languages?
- Read and write in their first, second and third languages?
- Do your goals for your child or children include active language learning (the ability to speak and write)?
- Do your goals for your child or children focus on passive language learning (the ability to listen and read)?

Being able to speak in two or more languages is the most common language goal. So, if you are a family who has reading and writing in two or more languages as your goal, you will need good planning coupled with a good strategy.

CONVERSATION STARTERS

Here are a few conversation starters for you and your family to answer, perhaps over a weekend family dinner:

1. **Multilinguals are not equally proficient in all their languages; it is common to favor one language over another depending on the situation.**

   - Which language do you feel strongest in and why?
   - Which language do you dream in?
   - Ask your family members which language they dream in.

2. **Our different languages are often the cues to our emotions.**

   - When you fight, or are angry or upset, which is your preferred language to express yourself in?
   - Ask your family members too.

3. **Many times, in multilingual families one partner cannot understand or speak the other partner's language.**

   - Can you and your partner both speak or understand each other's languages?

- Do you feel excluded if your partner speaks their native language with your children or can you follow what's being said?
- Ask your partner too.

4. **One challenge that many multilingual families face is excluding people from the conversation if you have friends or family over who may not understand one particular language being spoken.**

- Do you think it is necessary for the sake of consistency to speak to your kids in your native language, even when you have guests or family around who may not understand what you are saying at the risk of excluding them?
- Ask your family members how they feel about this too.

5. **Multilingual families face many challenges.**

- What is the hardest part about being a multilingual family?
- Ask your family members too.

6. **Multilingual families enjoy many opportunities.**

- What is the best part about being a multilingual family?
- Ask your family members too.

CHAPTER FOUR

THE MULTI-MOBILE FAMILY

· ·

THE DESIGN OF YOUR MOLA

"Unpack your bags and plant your trees. Live fully where you are, not where you've been or plan to go."

Ruth Van Reken

MY MULTI-MOBILE FAMILY

MAERSK HEADQUARTERS, COPENHAGEN, 2011:
Something is not right. I feel a wet sensation creeping over me. Despair fills my lungs and suddenly I cannot breathe. I look down at my stomach.

The baby.

"Mariam are you coming?" asks my boss, as he leads the Finance Team into the conference room for our 9 am, morning meeting. One by one all my colleagues grab their coffees and get up to go. It's month-end and we need to share progress.

"Go ahead, I'll be right there," I say as calmly as possible before slipping into the bathroom. It's then that I see the blood. Pouring out of me. Then a sharp pain. Is this what a miscarriage feels like? I'm only around eight weeks pregnant. Panic grips me, then fear.

I go back to my desk and call Martino and pray he picks up. His Maersk office is about 10 minutes away on Dampfærgevej, or as many Copenhagen expats call it, "Damn Far Away."

"Darling, I, I, I'm bleeding. The baby... I need to get to the hospital now. Can you meet me at Rigshospitalet?"

I have no car. Just a bike. But the thought of biking in such pain feels overwhelming. I go down to reception and ask Mads the security guard to call me a cab. I can count on my fingers the number of times I've taken a cab in Copenhagen, it's so expensive. But right now, I don't care how many kroner it costs. I can't think. I don't want to think. Surely, this can't be happening?

Two minutes later, I'm in the cab heading to the hospital. It is early morning but the canals of Christianshavn are full of life. Danes are biking to and fro as we pass the Metro Station, my favorite bakery Lagkagehuset is open and serving its warm Kanelstange (warm cinnamon bread) and the weather looks promising for an autumn day in late September. As we pull into Copenhagen's popular suburb of Østerbro, I think of how this whole Nordic city feels like home now, even though it took a while to adjust to life here after Berlin. Four years into our expat life in Denmark, these are the familiar streets where I feel the most safe and comfortable.

As I push open the doors of Rigshospitalet, I remember how just a few weeks ago I had heard the four words in Danish I had been waiting to hear for over two years.

"Tillykke! Du er gravid," (Congratulations! You are pregnant) the nurse had said to me with a huge grin. It had been a long time coming; this pregnancy was the result of major fertility battles including three failed IUIs (intrauterine inseminations) and one failed IVF (In-vitro fertilization). Martino and I had held hands and cried tears of joy when this second IVF had worked.

Was I going to lose this baby today?

I want to shout, to cry, to demand to be seen right away. But by now I know the Danish public health care system. I'm in Skadestue (emergency room) and will be seen as soon as possible. I see Martino walking towards me and collapse in his arms. He takes me to the bathroom. I'm still bleeding but thankfully there's no physical pain. Just my heart...

After what feels like the longest 30 minutes of my life, we are ushered into a medical exam room. Doctor Andersen looks at me kindly and starts talking to me in Danish. For a change I don't bother to correct him or ask him if he could speak English. All I want to know is if the baby is alright and I don't care which language I hear it in. Ironically, in this moment of stress and anguish, I speak better Danish than ever before as I sputter to explain what has happened.

"There's a heartbeat!" are the next words I hear, and I crane my neck to see the ultrasound. Sure enough there is a tiny flicker across the black and white screen. Relief floods through my brain. Martino squeezes my hand.

The baby is okay. No one knows why I have been bleeding but I'm still pregnant. Doctor Andersen grins. "It's hanging on, this is one stubborn baby!"

His words make me smile. We go home. I send an email to work calling in sick.

The next few weeks are traumatic. I experience two more threatened miscarriages. Each time I rush to Rigshospitalet, each time I check out fine. No one can explain what is causing the bleeding. Perhaps a surge of progesterone, due to the drugs and hormones pumped into me to increase my fertility. It doesn't matter. As long as the baby is fine and healthy. I am told I need to "take it easy" until I am through the tricky first trimester. Just when the morning sickness and nausea start to subside, and my pregnancy starts to stabilize, I am transferred out of the high-risk pregnancy care unit to the local midwife care in my neighborhood.

"Don't plan for anything too exciting for the next few months," says my assigned midwife at my first appointment.

But this is expat life and the only certainty is the uncertainty. Martino comes home one day with a box full of my favorite Danish pastries, so I know he has some good news to share.

"They're offering me a promotion; a posting to Singapore to look after South East Asia. It's a great opportunity! What do you think of having our first child born in Singapore? The medical care there is excellent. You could stop working, really take it easy and have a career break?" He sounds excited and full of hope, his eyes twinkle with anticipation.

I am quiet. For the past few months we had been hoping and praying to have a baby and planning our next move. It seemed like God had finally answered both our prayers but had done so simultaneously. Who am I to complain?

Still, I have so many fears of moving mid-pregnancy that I cannot begin to articulate even half of them. For the first time in my life, I don't feel like moving. I want my Scandinavian baby to be born here in this country that is now my home. I want to give birth at Rigshospitalet. I want to go for strolls with our baby beside Østerbro lake. I want to park the pram outside a café and let the baby take a nap outside the way my Danish friends do. Most of all, I want to use the maternity leave I am entitled to as a tax-paying Copenhagen resident – one year, fully paid, maternity leave. Gosh, I have worked so hard for this. I also want to go back to work after that year; the prospect of being a stay-at-home mom overwhelms me. For so many years my corporate career is what has defined me. The thought of giving it all up and arriving in Singapore pregnant and unemployed is terrifying.

We do some quick calculations. If Martino has to start his new job in Singapore in January 2012, I will be five months pregnant then. If this pregnancy continues. My body has failed me so many times, that I still keep thinking in 'if' mode.

The next few weeks I undergo several check-ups. My pregnancy is declared healthy, the baby is growing normally, and everything looks good. There are no more bleedings once I start the second trimester. I feel good, relaxed and on a professional high. I have completed a major project at work, ensuring that our business unit is EuroSox compliant according to the new European trading regulations of risk management and controls. The idea of handing in a resignation at the age of 29 is scary.

It is time to make a decision. One afternoon, as I take the S-tog train back from work, I notice a young Danish mother playing with her little daughter on her lap, scrunching her blonde hair into a tiny, bouncy ponytail. Clarity arrives for me as suddenly as the rain clouds gather when I get off at Svanemøllen Station and walk home.

"I don't care where I become a mother; as long as I become a mother,"
I say to Martino that cold, rainy November evening in our hyggeligt, *candlelit, Østerbro apartment.*

A new country, a new house, a new baby, a new job, a new continent, and possibly even a new career for me – the pattern of our mobile family was becoming messier; more colorful, more intricate and more complex. Our globally mobile lives now had a Danish layer sewn firmly on top and a few weeks later when I feel the first kicks to my stomach, I realize I am carrying the evidence of our Copenhagen lives, deep within me.

Leaving Copenhagen proves to be extremely tough. How do I say goodbye to my old life, while this new life is growing inside of me? But for the first time in my expat life, it finally feels like I'm taking much more with me than I'm leaving behind. Each time we move we seem to be taking a little something from each place we've lived in, but I still cannot foresee the end pattern; just richness, variety and a fascinating depth of color.

MOVING AS THE DESIGN OF YOUR MOLA

Your multi-mobile life becomes the design of your mola. The countries and cities you move to give your mola a unique design.

Essentially, the design of your mola tells the story of your mobile life. It shows you the different moves that make up your story. It is your *life by design*. The more you move, the more intricate and more complex the overall look of your mola becomes. Each place you move to adds something – a memory, a habit, a place, a food, a tradition, a friend, a baby, a certain perspective on things, an opinion – all of which you carry with you in some form or fashion. It guides your behavior and shapes your unique mola design.

By thinking about it in this way you celebrate new additions to your mola each time you move rather than feel that you're merely losing things. A mola can help you leave a place well, similar to the RAFT model as explained by David Pollock. He encourages globally mobile families to build their RAFT by leaving a place in peace (Reconciliation), affirming your experiences (Affirmation), honoring the goodbye (Farewell) and by thinking ahead (Think Destination). A mola feels like the final step in this process, whereby you 'stitch' in your latest experience and make it part of your mola design.

> **Essentially, the design of your mola tells the story of your mobile life. It shows you different moves that make up your story. It is your life by design.**

Sometimes, life as a globally mobile family can seem disjointed. You constantly start new lives in new locations, yet you cannot forget your old lives in the previous country you lived. Your career spans a few different continents, your children are born and raised in several different countries and you are constantly adding new dimensions and layers to your global identity.

What may seem like a disjointed or disconnected life on the move is actually forming a distinct design, just like a Guna woman stitching a mola using reverse appliqué, only to turn it over to reveal that the individual stitches have formed a unique design in the shape of an animal or a landscape. Globally mobile families are constantly taking their experiences from living around the world and 'sewing' them into the pattern of their mola. Each new country and each new experience means something else is added to your mola, as your design becomes clearer, more distinct and more formed.

Perhaps after leaving your home country of Canada and living for the past 10 years in the UAE, your mola design includes the representation in the shape of a falcon, that soars high and wide, travels between continents to look for food and yet always knows how to fly back home. Perhaps after moving to the Pacific Northwest in the United States, dominated by several mountain ranges like the Rocky Mountains and the Cascade Range, your mola design includes the shape of a mountain like Mount Rainier, symbolic of the obstacles you have had to conquer in your mobile life. Or perhaps, after moving to China with your multicultural family, you grow up feeling Asian and your mola design includes the shape of a panda, symbolic of your different races, nationalities and identities.

What designs do you see, when you turn your life mola over?

Globally mobile families are constantly taking their experiences from living around the world and sewing them into the pattern of their mola. Each new country and each new experience mean something else is added to your mola, as your design becomes clearer, more distinct and more formed. What design do you see, when you turn your life mola over?

Your design may depend on the type of moves you have made (international versus domestic or both) and the number of moves you have made. It may also depend on whether you started moving as a child (from the age of zero to eighteen) or as an adult (after the age of eighteen) or perhaps you have experienced mobility as both a child and an adult.

A GLOBALLY MOBILE CHILDHOOD (TCK)

Perhaps you first experienced mobility as a child who has lived around the world and moved often for your parent's career. Many such kids identify as Third Culture Kids. As a result of growing up in different cultures, many often feel as though they belong everywhere and nowhere. When these kids become adults, they transition into Adult Third Culture Kids (ATCKs).

"Learn to live in the paradox of this lifestyle. The blessings do not negate the challenges or vice versa. Affirm them both," advises Ruth Van Reken.

The best way to affirm both the blessings and the challenges of a mobile life is to start using the mola as a metaphor and as a way to become aware of all the elements in your story. Once you are aware of all the different layers in your story, you are able to honor and recognize them fully.

In the Guna culture, young girls are taught how to begin sewing a mola from the early age of nine or ten. Similarly, Third Culture Kids start building their metaphorical mola from an early age too. Each time they move, they add another layer to their mola design, which is ultimately another layer in their story. If a TCK moves from the United States to Turkey, he/she may add a Turkish layer to their mola; represented by Turkish sweets handed to them by a neighbor, their closest Turkish friend, summer memories in Istanbul or the smell of Turkish coffee. When they move again in a few years from Turkey to the Netherlands, they will 'stitch' a Dutch layer into their mola; perhaps represented by their first bike, their favorite Dutch phrases, a propensity to be direct in their communication, and a liking for herring. With each move, a

TCK is constantly adding some unique layers to their life story just like the layers are added to a mola, contributing to its exclusive pattern and design. Depending on how the transitions happen, it may be easy or difficult or even painful for a TCK to 'stitch' their different mola layers together.

This is so because moving often also involves loss, both tangible and intangible in the making of your life story. Loss of relationships, friendships, pets, languages and experiences are commonplace for globally mobile children. It is important to acknowledge these losses. Just like, the different layers are sewn and stitched into a mola, sewing and stitching these losses into your life story is the best way to ensure they continue to live on inside of you, no matter where you go. Diaries are often popular ways in which to remember a place or a time in one's life. While diaries allow an outlet for reflection and processing, a mola encourages one to focus on symbols, and sift through one's experiences to find representative motifs from potentially many years in one place.

When faced with a return to their home country (often their passport country), a TCK might try to hide their mola in order to fit in or simply because it may seem easier. Hiding your mola for different reasons means denying who you are and the diverse experiences which have shaped you along the way. Suppressing your mola in order to gain acceptance into your new environment can often feel painful. Wrong. Unfair. Unnatural. The mola as your life story is the most beautiful expression of who you are. Of the fabric you have used, of the different threads you have sewn with and of the design you have ultimately stitched together. The rich layers represent the richness in your life. Your mola is also unique to who you are and deserves to be worn proudly.

"Related to adjustment and adaptation issues is what I consider to be one of the trickiest internal dilemmas for parents of TCKs: to recognize, accept and celebrate that their children's cultural identity may end up very different from their own."
— Kristin Louise Duncombe.

"Parents of international kids have the critical task of preparing them for the 'hidden immigrant' reality, whether it is when they return to their passport country for a visit or as a 'permanent' relocation. In spite of the explosion in the last fifteen years of literature and resources for TCKs, the adaptation problems at repatriation, and sense of being a foreigner in one's 'own' country, remains one of the biggest challenges facing international families. Related to adjustment and adaptation issues is what I consider to be one of the trickiest internal dilemmas for parents of TCKs: to recognize, accept, and celebrate that their children's cultural identity may end up very different from their own," explains Kristin Louise Duncombe.

> **The mola as your life experience is the most beautiful expression of who you are. Of the fabric you have used, of the different threads you have sewn with and of the design you have ultimately stitched together. The rich layers represent the richness in your life. Your mola is also unique to who you are and deserves to be worn proudly.**

This is where a mola may help an international family understand and accept its different identities. There is the need to weave the home culture(s) into the fabric of your mola, before you start adding all the different layers on top. Parents of TCKs are busy making their own molas, but as Kristin points out, this may differ significantly from their children's mola, and the need to accept this is vital. Although you may have moved with your family to the same location, each family member may construct their mola differently. It is precisely this understanding that can help parents to accept and recognize their TCK child and the unique mola they build for themselves. This provides a great opportunity for family members to sit together and talk about their own mola. Having these mola discussions can provide a hugely rich opportunity for bonding and insight.

A GLOBALLY MOBILE ADULTHOOD (TCA)

If you experience mobility after the age of nineteen, as an adult, then your experience may be different from a globally mobile child. You would be a Third Culture Adult (TCA). The fabric of your mola (your home culture or cultures) will be quite settled and firm, but how much you build upon it and the different layers you add to it, may make your mola messy.

As an adult, you may be more conscious of the different layers you are adding onto your mola. Perhaps after living and working in Germany for seven years, you have adopted certain German habits in the workplace such as addressing your colleagues with the prefix of 'Herr' and 'Frau.' Perhaps you may find it difficult to integrate into the work culture in South Korea upon your return and may struggle with the hierarchical workplace and the etiquettes it demands. Perhaps after working in the Asian economy of Singapore, you find the lack of transparency in Nigeria difficult to handle. Perhaps after working in Denmark where showing off at the workplace is highly frowned upon, you struggle to thrive in Italy, where connections and who you know is the key to career advancement.

Adults who move around may also feel that because they have enjoyed a relatively stable childhood, they know where they come from and have more formulated identities – and they may not be as 'confused' about where to call 'home' or from where they draw their sense of belonging. A mola can help you see exactly how your international experiences have shaped you and how the layers you have added, give shape and meaning to the pattern of your mobile life. Creating a mola in cloth, in paint, on paper, as a collage or in some kind of graphic format is a tangible way to understand how living abroad has shaped you and your ideals.

A GLOBALLY MOBILE CHILDHOOD AND ADULTHOOD

What if you have led both a globally mobile childhood and adulthood? If mobility continues from childhood to adulthood, this is where your mola becomes extremely interesting, because it is messy to chart out.

As someone who grew up as an expat child, and is now an ATCK and a mother to two expat kids herself, I never know which box to tick, because they all seem to apply to me:

- Globally mobile childhood (TCK): ✔

- Repatriation to passport country: ✔
- ATCK: ✔
- Multicultural Marriage with a CCK: ✔
- Multilingual Family: ✔
- Raising Cross-Cultural Kids all over the world: ✔

This is why after living in nine countries, my mobile life is messy. I sometimes don't know or cannot separate where one cultural influence ends and the other begins. This is also why charting out my MOLA Family helps in understanding and integrating these diverse experiences from both childhood and adulthood. It also helps me to see things from both angles: the point of view of the globally mobile kid and the point of view of the globally mobile adult with her own kids. In short by using the mola as a metaphor, I am able to see the story of my life clearly.

"By feeling connected to various cultures and places, your child might not develop a strong sense of belonging to one particular one. Like the mola, they will weave their own tapestry of cultures that eventually becomes a reflection of themselves. And, undoubtedly, they will feel a very strong sense of belonging to those who have done the same," says Valérie Besanceney as she highlights the shared experience.

"By feeling connected to various cultures and places, your child might not develop a strong sense of belonging to one particular one. Like the mola, they will weave their own tapestry of cultures that eventually becomes a reflection of themselves."

— Valérie Besanceney.

As Valérie points out, the MOLA is a good tool for both parents and children to chart out their family experiences, identities and paths. A MOLA Family is constantly developing, expanding and adding new layers.

DEFINITIONS AND EXAMPLES OF MULTI-MOBILE FAMILIES

A multi-mobile family is one which moves more than once, either internationally or domestically or both. Multi-mobile families thus typically include expatriate families, missionary families, military families and diplomatic families. It may also include families who migrate, such as refugee families or immigrant families because even though their intention may only be to migrate just once, the reality in many cases is that they also move more than once.

Mobile families may make only two moves or may make seven – this only affects the degree of complexity of their mola and how intricate its pattern. Multi-mobile families often relocate due to work assignments for the parents which is a common trend worldwide with the globalization of the workforce, the emergence of a global labor market, and the fierce war for talent, where scarce skills migrate around the world to where they are most in demand.

MEET THE MOLA FAMILIES

There are many different types of MOLA Families who are multi-mobile.

An Expat Family Who Moves Internationally

Eva and her husband are both Portuguese. As an expat couple they have lived in Scotland and the UAE, while both their children were born in Edinburgh.

"I feel that I don't belong anywhere. My boys feel they belong everywhere. They proudly wear their kilt and say Scottish poems, they adore Portuguese food and believe Dubai is home. But I am the contrary; I no longer identify myself with Portugal, I miss Scotland dearly and I don't fit in Dubai. I wish I had their optimism," says Eva.

A Diplomatic Family Who Moves Internationally and Domestically

Clara is part of a British diplomatic family and was born in Cuba. She has led a globally mobile childhood and adulthood as an ATCK and has lived in Cuba, the UK (several places including London), Philippines, Nigeria, Venezuela, Gibraltar, Spain, New Zealand, Jamaica, Pakistan, St. Lucia and South Africa. Her two children were born in the UK, to where she currently has repatriated.

"I am finding it hard now to reconcile being English with what our country has become. I am not proud of my country or heritage at the moment with Brexit, but on the other hand think it is important for my children to have some sort of sense of identity and roots," explains Clara.

A Family Who Moves Domestically and Internationally

Naomi and her husband are both American. Naomi grew up in Omaha, Nebraska, but has since moved multiple times with her family – both domestically and internationally. Her mobile life has taken her family all around the United States (Georgia, Ohio,

Florida, Virginia and Nebraska), and her family has also moved abroad to India and Singapore.

"Our children are such 'troopers' when it comes to our frequent moves, and not until they reached their teenage years, did we start to see the real evidence of grief and loss. It manifests itself daily in our lives and feels almost like a low cloud that covers or masks our joy and our ability to love and bond to a new location or place," explains Naomi.

A Missionary Family Who Moves Internationally

Marilyn grew up in an American missionary family and thus spent her childhood in Pakistan. As a missionary TCK American kid, Marilyn learned quickly how to act as a bridge between cultures. She then continued to raise her own family in Pakistan, Egypt and the United States. She and her husband have recently moved to Kurdistan, Iraq, for work.

"Our family has moved so much that finding a true sense of belonging is incredibly difficult both individually and as a family unit. We were always the family that left. As a mixture of extroverts and introverts, we all respond differently to this challenge. It has made us deeply empathetic to the situation of refugees and displaced people, and we respond by opening up our home to those who also find themselves between worlds. I think what I am incredibly grateful for is the deep sense of empathy all of us have to the one who is the other," explains Marilyn.

An Immigrant Family Who Moves Internationally

Zareen and her husband are both from Pakistan. They made plans to migrate to the United States with their two sons in search of a better future, but their immigration journey first took them to Canada. After living and working in Edmonton for five years, their paperwork for US immigration finally came through and the family of four then immigrated to the United States.

"Our two sons were nine and seven years old when we left Pakistan. But they have never been back since, because we were busy building new lives for ourselves first in Edmonton, then in Houston. My husband struggled to find a job in his industry (engineering) and settled for a career as an insurance salesman. I finished my medical degree in Pakistan, but never had a chance to become a doctor in the United States. I had to start earning right away to support our family and took a job as a saleswoman in a big department store. Immigration to the US has obviously opened up doors for our sons now 33 and 31; one has become a doctor, the other an accountant. Home for them is definitely Texas, but I do wish we had kept their connection to Pakistan alive," explains Zareen.

A Jewish Family Who Moves Internationally Struggles with Identity

Daniela was born in Argentina and holds Israeli nationality. Her husband was born in Israel and also holds Belgian nationality. As a family with four kids they have lived in Israel, Belgium and the United States.

"I believe that the identity part is the most challenging for us. It is very clear that wherever you live has a strong meaning. Living in Israel as Israelis is a very distinguished identity, it has the benefit of a strong sense of belonging. When you leave Israel, you lose that. In Europe, it was hard to be Jewish. At times, we had to ask the kids to hide their identity, it was too dangerous. In Boston, it was a pleasant surprise to be allowed to express all parts of our identity, but by then some of my kids had adopted a more international identity. So in the end, there is no one clear identity that is stable and represents all the members of our family. It is hard to feel at times that your kids are uncomfortable with different parts of their identity," explains Daniela.

A Refugee Family Who Moves Internationally

Zaitoona grew up in an Afghani family in Jalalabad who fled their native Afghanistan at the time of the Soviet invasion in the early 90s. As a refugee family, the first country they fled to was neighboring Pakistan. Zaitoona remembers living in a refugee camp in Peshawar, in Pakistan's Northern Areas. After a few years, Zaitoona's family fled to Denmark, where they were granted asylum as refugees by the social welfare system. She speaks fluent Danish and her husband is half Danish/half Palestinian and was born and raised in Denmark as a CCK. Together, they have three kids of their own who have lived in Denmark and experienced an international move to Qatar for an expat posting.

"Moving to Doha as expats was a very different experience than moving as refugees. Our life in Qatar was about embracing a new country, a new lifestyle, new opportunities and exposing the kids to an international school and environment. My kids' experience

> of moving as expat kids was very different to my own experience
> of moving as a refugee kid!" says Zaitoona.

MOVING AS A CHOICE VERSUS MOVING FOR SAFETY AND PROSPERITY

The different types of MOLA Families make it clear that moving is sometimes a choice, but sometimes it is the last desperate attempt in search of safe shores. Moving as an expat family and going from one expat assignment to another is very different from moving as a refugee family from place to place, applying for asylum.

Our moving vocabulary is made up of different terms – to immigrate, to migrate, to flee, to rotate, to expatriate, to seek refuge or the chance to build a better future. As a result, multi-mobile families sometimes feel that because they all move under different circumstances with varying motives and rationales, it is hard to understand the commonalities that they share as a result of all their moves.

In this book, I present the commonality of the idea that regardless of how you move, or why you move, or where you move to, if you are a multi-mobile family, you are building a mola. And in doing so, you face certain challenges and enjoy unique opportunities.

THE CHALLENGES AND OPPORTUNITIES OF A MULTI-MOBILE FAMILY – OUR EXPERTS ADVISE

Being a multi-mobile family, regardless of type (expatriate, immigrant, missionary, military, diplomatic) brings forth its own unique challenges and opportunities. I collected data from hundreds of international families through *The Mobile Family Survey* in 2018, through which participants shared their experiences from around the world. I chose a few examples of challenges faced by multi-mobile families and asked my team of three mobility experts to offer some advice and solutions.

A Swedish/Danish ATCK Mother and a Uruguayan/Italian Father Raise a Family in Kenya

Taina was born in Belgium and holds dual Danish and Swedish citizenship. She grew up as a TCK, so has lived all around the world including Belgium, Zimbabwe, Luxembourg, Malawi, Tanzania, UK, Ireland, USA, France, Costa Rica, Switzerland, Mali, DR Congo and Kenya. Her partner was born and raised in Uruguay and holds dual Uruguayan and Italian citizenship. Together as a couple they currently live in Nairobi, Kenya, where they are raising their two-year-old daughter, who was born in Sweden. Their biggest challenge as a family is identifying their sense of home.

"I would like my daughter to grow up with a stronger Danish/ Swedish identity and background than I did. I grew up outside both of my native countries which has been bittersweet. Sweet because I have experienced the world from the moment I was born, and this has opened up my eyes and my ability to relate, adapt, understand and work. However, bitter in the sense that it has also led to a loss of identity, not being able to speak either mother tongue perfectly and without an accent that identifies me as either a Swede or a Dane. I would like my daughter to identify more with her countries of origin, but as her nationality is even more diluted than mine, because we now have Uruguay and Italy in the mix, this will be even more difficult. As a result, I guess I am trying to make our home as positive as I can, one that she can identify her background with and relate to, one with as much positive influence from her four nationalities as possible, while living in a country that has nothing to do with them," explains Taina.

* * *

Q: HOW CAN TAINA INSTILL A STRONG SENSE OF IDENTITY IN HER DAUGHTER WHICH ENCAPSULATES HER DIVERSE BACKGROUND?

A: **Expert Ruth Van Reken has some advice for Taina on her unique identity:**

Dear Taina,

I commend your desire to make your home a safe, nurturing place that includes aspects of your daughter's national heritages. You offer her a great beginning towards developing a strong sense of identity. Choosing which languages, you and your partner speak with her at home can also be part of that gift and help her connect to your extended families.

Another way you can help is to re-frame your story slightly. Never forget that while you *are* a Swede/Dane, you *also* grew up as a cross-cultural kid (CCK) – someone who meaningfully interacts with different cultural worlds during childhood. Often this experience results in the paradoxical outcome you describe as "bittersweet" – your sense of belonging 'everywhere and nowhere.' In a typically either/or world, you likely felt forced to choose between these two realities.

If, instead, you realize that others who also grew up as CCKs share the same feeling of "Who am I, really?" You will discover the amazing fact that you belong to a group who truly understand your story. Then you can help your CCK daughter celebrate her "all of the above" story too. Best of all, by normalizing your daughter's culturally complex heritage, you can celebrate that richness while not being afraid to add fresh discoveries from each new place and people you encounter. One day your daughter will thank you for her rich identity!

Best,
Ruth

A French Mother and a Portuguese Father Raise CCKs in Germany

Annabelle is French, while her husband is Portuguese. Both parents are multilingual, speaking French, English, German, Portuguese and Spanish. Their first child was born in the UK and their second born in Germany. They are currently raising their multicultural and multilingual family in Germany. Their number one challenge is the fact that home is a different place for each family member.

"Our children's sense of home is what matters to me the most right now. I worry they will not know what home is. Our oldest (eight years old) gets asked all the time where she is from. She panicked the first few times as she had no idea what to answer. She is a happy multilingual switching effortlessly between languages. But home and 'where are you from' is not something she can handle right now. We are trying to develop a sense of Europe and a European identity. But not many people understand that," explains Annabelle.

In spite of the challenges Annabelle is appreciative that her children are growing up with a global outlook.

"I want my children to understand that they are not confined to their passport or their nationality or their languages. The world is big, and they should be looking out instead of in. We make a conscious effort to show them the world through books, travel, friendships, food etc.," says Annabelle.

° ° °

Q: HOW CAN ANNABELLE TEACH HER DAUGHTER TO GIVE AN ANSWER TO WHERE SHE IS FROM?

A: Expert Kristin Louise Duncombe has some advice for Annabelle on this topic:

Dear Annabelle,

While it is true that the world is big, and one is not confined to any particular place, it is important to consider where your child is developmentally. Eight years "old" is still very young to formulate answers to complicated questions about home and identity.

To help your daughter feel calm, as opposed to panicked, when asked questions about where she is from, it would be useful to provide some answers *for* her, knowing that this eventually gives her something to rebel against. The reality is that young kids are very identified with their parents until they begin the differentiation process that comes with adolescence and young adulthood.

Talking openly with your daughter about the complexity of multiple languages and cultures – and providing her a clear idea of where you consider home and why, will help her identify her own answers.

We swaddle babies to prevent them from flailing, so as to help them feel safe. Telling your daughter "this is where I am from and how I answer, and this is where your dad is from and how he answers," and then asking her if she would like to brainstorm some of her possible answers, is akin to swaddling. It will help her feel that there *are* parameters and that the world is not so big that she will just get swallowed up in it.

Best,
Kristin

A Guatemalan ATCK Helps her Daughter to Explore her Multiple Identities

Alice was born in Guatemala and holds citizenship from Panama and the United States. Her husband is American with an Italian background. Alice has lived in Guatemala, Panama, the United States, France, Italy and Costa Rica. In 2018 they were living with their seven-year-old daughter, a US Citizen, in Costa Rica, although they would soon move back to the United States. Reconciling multiple identities in their family is what Alice finds the biggest challenge.

"For UN day at school, I was excited to show my daughter a picture of me in a traditional Guatemalan outfit and even more excited because I had it so she could wear it. She said it was nice, but she wanted to wear a US shirt with a traditional Costa Rican skirt instead, to really represent where she's from. Mind you, she's not

Costa Rican but since we live here she thinks that's also part of her identity. I said fine and she was not the only kid with random mixed (confused) attire at her international school!" explains Alice.

o o o

Q: HOW CAN ALICE HELP HER DAUGHTER FIND A WAY TO OWN HER MULTIPLE IDENTITIES?

A: **Expert Valérie Besanceney has some advice for Alice on helping children with multiple identities:**

Dear Alice,

Children should be encouraged to develop a sense of belonging to whichever culture or country they identify with, which may not necessarily be the ones their parents feel they are "supposed to" feel connected to.

You can help your daughter by acknowledging that Costa Rica truly is part of her identity now. Telling a child that they have a random or confused interpretation of culture undermines and undervalues the child's evolving sense of identity. If the parent assumes the child is confused, the child will likely feel confused.

Alice, your daughter is actually conveying a very strong message by appreciating your traditional Guatemalan outfit but opting for two pieces of clothing that resonate with her. She clearly already has a strong sense of identity with the United States and now with Costa Rica as well.

Perhaps you can suggest a subtle Guatemalan or Italian accessory like a hair clip or necklace to communicate that these cultures are also a part of her rich heritage. If you encourage her to own each culture and wear all of it with a strong sense of pride, your daughter will develop a stronger sense of identity.

Best,
Valérie

PRACTICAL CHALLENGES AND OPPORTUNITIES

Many respondents highlighted several practical challenges that moving had meant for them. Amongst these were:

- Dealing with spousal employment or the difficulty for the spouse to be gainfully employed (especially in diplomatic circles where spouses are not allowed to work on a diplomatic passport).
- Transitioning their children through different school systems (British, International Baccalaureate, American system, and so on).
- Saving up for retirement after working overseas and in many cases not qualifying for social security benefits in their passport country, and not knowing which country to retire to.
- Struggling to maintain friendships over different continents or developing a sense of community or depth in relationships due to a mobile lifestyle.
- Struggling to integrate into their host country culture, particularly if it is a homogenous culture and not a multicultural or international environment.
- Dealing with the dynamics of a split family, where often the husband goes to work abroad while the wife and kids remain in their home country.

However, respondents also identified several opportunities and advantages they enjoy as a result of being a mobile family, such as:

- Enjoying access to many different cultures.
- Practicing empathy and helping to communicate across boundaries.
- Increased opportunities for world travel.
- Enjoying international friendships.
- Raising resilient and adaptable children whose world view is all-encompassing.
- Reaping benefits of a tighter nuclear family, because "home is wherever we are all together."
- Living in a safe environment, if the reason for leaving the home country was war, instability or a high crime rate.

YOUR MOLA TOOLBOX:
L IS FOR LAYER

When I left Denmark, I had subconsciously added a Danish layer to my mola without realizing it. But while the Danish layer covered the other layers underneath, my German layer, my American layer, my British layer and my Pakistani layer had the ability to shine through whenever I needed them to. Cheering myself up on a bad day meant cooking *daal chawal* (white rice with lentils) no matter where I was. Some layers remain hidden, underneath your surface, but the old layers still form part of who you are. And you can expose them or re-activate them easily, by cutting through your mola to reveal the richness that lies below the surface.

I built up all my different layers at a subconscious level. But it was only when I embraced all the layers consciously through my mola did I begin to understand my reaction to news and events. I found that sometimes my different layers caused a lot of internal conflict within me. When I moved back to the United States a few months after 9/11, I struggled to relate my Muslim identity to the fact that the country I was living in was responsible for civilian deaths in Pakistan due to the bombing of neighboring Afghanistan and the raids to locate Osama Bin Laden. Perhaps this was also the reason I found myself wearing fewer *shalwar kameezes* during my time in the States, to lessen the occasions I marked myself as the 'other.'

Years later, when the Danish cartoon controversy regarding the Prophet Muhammad made headlines, I felt conflicted between my Pakistani self, my religious beliefs and my staunch belief in freedom of speech while living in Copenhagen. Sometimes my different layers didn't stitch a pattern cohesively but rather vied for attention and space on my mola. Sometimes they provoked complex reactions in me, that were multidimensional and difficult to explain to others.

Some layers remain hidden, underneath the surface, but the old layers still form part of who you are. And you can expose them or re-activate them easily, by cutting through your mola to reveal the richness that lies below the surface.

In the years that have passed, my Danish layer is now overlaid by my Singaporean layer, my UAE layer and my Ghanaian layer. I have continued building layers into my mola, with each move. But my Danish layer is still present; it's that Copenhagen painting in my room, that Viking Map of Scandinavia in my living room, the Royal Copenhagen coffee mugs, my acquired taste for herring, my liking for Danish crime TV series (in their original language!) and my notions of the ideal work/life balance which have shaped my interests and opinions even today. When I hear Danish being spoken, I gravitate to the sounds of a language that represents familiarity and comfort.

Therefore, in my framework of a MOLA Family, L stands for Layer. Once you have your fabric and your thread, it is time to start creating your MOLA Family by layering your international and domestic moves one on top of the other but allowing them to show in a piece of jewelry, in the words that you use or the food that you eat.

LAYERING YOUR MOVES INTO YOUR MOLA FAMILY

If you think of all the moves you make as the different layers of your mola, it helps you to see what you are building over time. It's a cumulative process; one which is continuous and changing.

When you add a layer onto your mola, what exactly are you adding? You could be adding one or several different elements, such as:

- The positive experiences from the move
- The negative experiences from the move
- The relationships you fostered
- The friends you gained
- The community you were a part of
- The baby you had while living there
- The job you worked at
- The work habits you adopted

- The local mannerisms you adopted
- The cultural norms you adopted
- The food you ate and cooked
- The language you heard every day
- The currency you shopped in
- The house/apartment/condo you lived in
- The neighbors you had
- The clubs and activities you were a part of
- The pet you had while living there
- The daily frustrations you experienced
- The local issues which affected you (pollution, high taxes, gender inequality, gun control, poverty etc.).

You may find it really difficult to 'stitch' certain things from the above list into your mola. For instance, the aspects of a new country you struggled to adapt to may be one of these. Perhaps you are from Japan and struggled with the way the Dutch were so direct, when you lived in the Netherlands. You thought it rude when they gave you their unfiltered opinions on how you should do things while living in their country. Perhaps as a Swede you felt unsafe going out alone as a female while living in Bangalore amidst India's prevalent rape culture. These experiences don't end when we leave a country; they continue to mold us and shape us long after we have left a certain place. It is a good idea not to forget about them or underestimate their influence on you and the way you communicate or present yourselves going forward. This is why it is important to 'stitch' even unpleasant experiences into your mola because often these have left a mark on you and determined the pattern of your mola. Sometimes these remain hidden in our mola layers, but a certain event or situation could trigger these to shine through.

Sometimes our layers overlap. To my joy I realize that in my MOLA Family, our Italian and Pakistani layers converge on the importance of family gatherings, food as the ultimate comfort and respect for the older generation. It is clear that any celebration will involve family and food.

You may notice this too. Making your MOLA Family means dissecting and examining your different layers. Figuring out if they are all equal, or if some layers are thicker, while others are thinner. Understanding why although you are Australian born and bred, your Lebanese immigrant layer is at the heart of important decisions that you make.

When you layer your MOLA Family together, you are drawing on the experiences of not just yourself but your whole family. This means you are adding on a lot of complexity in thoughts, emotions, feelings, relationships and experiences. Often times, if you move as a family of four from Turkey to China, each individual family member will experience the move in different ways. How do you represent this in your mola?

THE FIVE RULES FOR GLOBALLY MOBILE FAMILIES

1. REMEMBER, THE SAME INTERNATIONAL MOVE WILL SHAPE YOUR FAMILY MEMBERS DIFFERENTLY

A mobile family experiences the same move, but each family member may process the move differently. Perhaps the father in the family is excited about the move and his new job opportunity, while his wife is apprehensive to give up her career. Perhaps their seven-year-old does not want to say goodbye to her friends at school, but her two-year-old brother is too young to grasp the move. Ruth Van Reken advises parents to "understand the normal stages of any transition and common responses of each stage. Transition involves loss as well as potential gain. Recognize each family member may be going through the stages of grief – denial, anger, depression, bargaining and acceptance – at different rates. Be patient in the process."

2. GIVE YOUR CHILDREN THE TOOLBOX TO HANDLE TRANSITIONS

Each mobile family needs to develop their own toolbox on how to help their children handle transition. Kristin Louise Duncombe says, "I recommend that parents pay attention to three main areas where kids often need help facing loss. The first is attachment. Closure is essential to moving forward adaptively, and this will require parents to create or facilitate rituals or ceremonies to say goodbye. This can be as straightforward as a goodbye party, or it can be more obscure, like making a list of everything that their child will miss and establishing ways to acknowledge letting go of those things. The second area that requires attention is helping kids deal with the loss of their sense of competence. It is critical for parents to find age-appropriate ways for their kids to develop a sense of self-efficacy in the new country. This can be as simple as learning to answer the phone in the local language, or as complex as allowing older children to navigate public transport and move around the new city on their own. Finally, a move also creates a loss of control for many kids, so it is important to identify ways to let them get involved in decision-making, if and when appropriate. This could be as simple as being in charge of packing one box of special stuff, or as complex as weighing in on what neighborhood to live in in the new country."

3. EMPHASIZE PORTABLE TRADITIONS IN YOUR FAMILY LIFE

When you live a life on the move, it can be easy to be swept up in a storm of instability. One of the best strategies for mobile families is to define and emphasize the portable traditions in your family life – the things you do together as a family no matter where you live. Valérie Besanceney advises, "Have certain traditions move with you. Bringing along portable traditions will allow them to feel a sense of belonging wherever they may go. This may be singing the same bedtime songs wherever you are, having a weekly game night or routinely inviting friends to a traditional meal (also a perfect opportunity to get to know new friends in your new destination better). When everything else changes, bringing along a sense of continuity can be really stabilizing."

4. COMFORT BEFORE YOU ENCOURAGE

As parents, our instinct can always be to try to protect our kids. Ruth Van Reken advises, "Never try to talk your children out of what they are feeling. Comfort before you encourage." Valérie Besanceney agrees. She explains that "as children develop their sense of identity and belonging, they are still in the process of articulating their thoughts and emotions. As adults we often want to 'fix' things that hurt our children, but we cannot 'fix' feelings. We can only provide them with tools to recognize and process their emotions. This will benefit them infinitely more than ensuring that everything will be okay."

5. UNPACK YOUR BAGS, PLANT YOUR TREES AND BUILD YOUR MOLA

The rule here is to live fully wherever you go. Ruth Van Reken advises mobile families to form those deep connections with their communities and to live in the moment even if you know you only have two or three years in a certain place. In addition to unpacking your bags and planting your trees, mobile families can use the MOLA as a concept and a tool to help process all the different experiences and layers they build up as part of their global identities. A MOLA is the perfect tool to make sense of this life lived on the move, as you see what you are building. What part of your mola might need repairing. What part was difficult to sew on. Which threads you have used. How stable your fabric is. What colors you have used. What design you have created.

CHAPTER SUMMARY

1. Your multi-mobile background forms the design of your mola. The different countries, cities and states that you move to ultimately stitch together the design of your mola.

2. Your mola design (your story) may depend on the types of moves you have made; whether you have moved as an expat family, a military family, an immigrant family, a missionary family or a refugee family. It may also depend on the number of moves you have made and whether you started moving as a child, as an adult or both. Regardless of the reasons and motivations for moving, all multi-mobile families are busy making a mola.

3. Some of the big challenges of multi-mobile families include fostering a sense of identity, developing a sense of belonging, dealing with culture clash, not being able to identify where home is and to raise children who can adapt and thrive amidst transitions. Some of the big opportunities enjoyed by multi-mobile families are: a global outlook, access to many cultures, increased resilience and adaptability in the face of change, and the chance to break down barriers and boundaries.

4. In your MOLA toolbox, L stands for Layer. In creating a MOLA Family, multi-mobile families layer their international and domestic moves on top of the other to reveal a distinct design.

5. To layer your moves into your MOLA Family, it is important to understand that family members may react and respond differently to the same move, to give your children a toolbox to handle transition, to emphasize portable traditions in your family life, to comfort before you encourage and to live fully no matter where you go.

ACTIVITY: CHART YOUR GLOBAL MOBILITY DESIGN AND ITS IMPACT ON YOUR MOLA FAMILY

It's time for you as a family to chart the moves you have made as a mobile family and see what design your MOLA shows.

Chart Your Global Mobility

Answer the following questions:

1. Where have you lived as a family? Please list all the different cities, states and countries below.

2. How many moves (domestic and international) have you made?

3. How many layers does your mola have? Name each layer with the city or country you associate it with.

Then answer the following questions for each country or new city you have moved to in the table opposite:

4. What were the key positive and negative experiences in each place?

5. What were your best/worst memories in each place?

6. What were some key habits you developed after living in each place?

7. What memorabilia did you take with you from each location that is important to you?

8. What are your associations with each place when you look back?

Country	Key positive experience	Key negative experience	Best memory	Worst memory	Key habits developed	Memorabilia taken when you left	Key association with the place
Country 1							
Country 2							
Country 3							
Country 4							
Country 5							
Country 6							
Country 7							

For some help, here are my answers. This is what my mola looks like for the moves I have made with my MOLA Family:

Country	Key positive experience	Key negative experience	Best memory	Worst memory
Denmark	Finding work as an expat spouse.	Experiencing infertility abroad without close family for support.	Learning I was pregnant.	Suffering three threatened miscarriages.
Singapore	Becoming a mother for the first time.	Being hospitalized for pre-eclampsia shortly after giving birth.	Having my wallet returned by a cab driver, after accidentally leaving it behind in the cab.	Daughter suffering Hand, Foot and Mouth disease and both of us in quarantine for two weeks.
UAE	Learning from the desert how to practice mindfulness.	Not being able to practice freedom of speech.	The day our son was born in Dubai.	Facing a sudden job loss for my husband due to a reorganization in the company.

Key habits developed	Memorabilia taken when you left	Key association with the place
To go outside no matter what the weather (rain, sun, sleet, snow etc.).	Maps, books, Scandinavian dining table, Royal Copenhagen mugs, a book by Hans Christian Andersen.	Living by the sea, working for a shipping company, Copenhagen harbor, many canals running through the city = proximity to water.
Speaking Singlish.	A Peranakan elephant, colonial map of Singapore, a Singapore sketchbook, daughter's first cheongsam (Chinese dress) and chopsticks.	The value of multiculturalism and how to live in a multicultural society.
Understanding and embracing a place for what it is and not judging it by wrong standards. Once I understood Bedouin culture, I understood the UAE culture.	Lamps, lanterns, paintings of the Dubai skyline, a hand of Fatima necklace for protection and sand from the desert.	The desert nomads and me as a global nomad had a lot in common, Entrepreneurship: how to dream big and reach high for your goals.

DESIGN OF YOUR MOLA:

What design starts to emerge when you join all the different layers of your mola together? Do you see a landscape emerge? Or perhaps an animal? Or perhaps a building? Or something else?

When I join all these layers of my mola together, slowly some designs start to emerge:

Pattern 1: Living by the sea makes me happy and free. A lot of my expat family life takes place by the sea (the Indian Ocean, the Arabian Sea, the Atlantic, and the South China Sea). THE SEA

Pattern 2: Landscapes figure prominently in my mola than particular buildings or architecture. The Arabian Desert with its sand dunes becomes synonymous with home. THE DESERT

Pattern 3: Shapes, geography and continents figure greatly in my mola. CONTINENTS

Where I have Lived

	Germany	Denmark	Singapore	UAE	Ghana
What Represents my time there	Brandenburg Gate	The Copenhagen harbor	A Chinese dragon	Arabian desert/sand dunes	Colorful kente cloth fabric
	Eagle (national symbol)	Canals	Red lanterns	Palm trees	
		The 'Dannebrog' (Red and white Danish flag)	An orchid (Singapore's national flower)	Falcon	

Once you can begin to identify the major themes in your mola design, you can start to picture your mola design. This is how you can start to visualize the life you are creating by design. Ultimately, figuring out the design of your mola is about symbolism. Everything that you put on your mola stands for something: a feeling, an experience, an attachment but also your perspective and state of mind. For example, if I put the desert or sand dunes on my mola design, it reflects the peaceful state of mind that I experienced whenever I visited the desert, which is symbolic of me being at peace with my messy mobile life.

When I lived in Singapore, my daughter Mina was born in the year of the dragon, making her a "dragon baby" as the locals called her, which is considered to be very lucky. In Chinese astrology, the dragon zodiac represents character traits such as being driven, unafraid of challenges and willing to take risks. For me these are all crucial elements for a successful MOLA Family.

When I moved to Ghana, I was fascinated by the colorful kente cloth fabric worn here. I embraced the colorful local dressing style whole-heartedly, which is symbolic of me embracing each country I live in and making it a part of who I am.

CONVERSATION STARTERS

Here are a few conversation starters for you and your family to answer, perhaps over a weekend family dinner:

1. **When you are trying to sew/envisage the different layers of your MOLA Family together, it is often easier to sew in positive experiences and harder to sew in difficult transitions.**

    - Take turns with each family member to discuss what parts of your globally mobile lifestyle have been easy to stitch in.
    - What parts have been hard to incorporate and why?

2. **Some layers in your mola are thick, while others may be thinner. Sometimes it is to do with the amount of time we spend in a particular place.**

    - Take turns with each family member to discuss which layers in your mola are thick and why.
    - Which layers are thin and why?

3. **Our moves form the layers of our MOLA Family. Sometimes cutting through to reveal the richness underneath is necessary but painful.**

- Take turns with your family members to discuss in which social situations you feel forced to cut through your mola layers. At a job interview? When you meet somebody new? When you return to your home (passport) country for a visit? When you repatriated to your home country?

CHAPTER FIVE

A MOLA FAMILY IS BORN

. . . .

"Adventure isn't hanging on a rope off the side of a mountain. Adventure is an attitude that we must apply to the day to day obstacles in life."

John Amatt

MY MOLA FAMILY

MAKOLA MARKET, ACCRA, GHANA 2018:

I close my eyes, but I still can't block out the incessant noise from people, traffic and livestock. As soon as the traffic light turns red, our car comes to a screeching halt on a road littered with rubbish on each side. Then hawkers, beggars and young kids start flowing left and right in a coordinated traffic flow all of their own. Women wearing brightly colored African fabrics, carry babies on their backs and balance impressively-high towering baskets on their heads. Baskets full of nuts, biscuits, cool drinks, chocolate and local snacks like plantain chips and waakye (a Ghanaian dish of cooked rice and beans). A few knock on my window when they see me. Kids not older than ten or twelve are selling wallets, watches and laundry detergent.

Even though I am in my second month of living in West Africa, I can't help but stare and marvel at their ability to balance huge weights on their heads, without looking down. They carry their baskets proudly like crowns. Scientific research has proven that it is easier to carry heavy loads on our heads than it is in our hands. Of course, by carrying what they are selling on their heads, these hawkers have their hands free to accept money and give out change to passing cars.

"Ma'am, we are here!" announces Daniel, my local driver. Thanks to him, I have been learning some key phrases of the local Akan language known as Twi which is widely spoken in this region of Ghana.

Here means Accra's famous Makola Market. It is noisy and insistent, teeming with people and goods sprawled over the sidewalk like an open-air garage sale that just spills out into the roads. Baskets full of sea-snails, fresh fish and huge yams are being sold on one end, richly colored kente cloth, textile, shoes and wallets on the other end, with just about everything in between.

As I step out, I realize I need to keep up with the rhythm of this market. It is fast-paced, and there is a certain flow as women of all ages whizz past me, carrying peanuts, potatoes, hair brushes, and cold drinks on top of their heads. I put my phone inside my purse and start navigating this never-ending maze and realize I need to tread carefully so as not to knock a banana off the stack a vendor is transporting, or bump into a pile of fabrics four feet high.

"Obroni! Obroni!" shout a couple of the hawkers in Twi as they walk past me. One entices me to look at his ware of sunglasses. I have learned not to be offended when I hear this term being directed at me, for although it means foreigner *or used to refer to someone with lighter skin, I know it is not necessarily meant as a racial slur but more an acknowledgment of my 'otherness.' I smile politely and say* "me daa se" *(thank you).*

My attention is riveted by the women carrying huge, empty silver trays on their head. How are they balancing these massive trays on their heads without falling over? A quick glance down to see you don't step in a puddle or a pothole, and the whole thing would come tumbling down.

Daniel sees my look of amazement and comes over to explain:

"This young woman is called a 'kayayoo', a female head porter who carries other people's loads on her head for a fee."

"Oh! So, I can do some shopping in the market and then pay her to carry it for me? How much would she earn by doing this?"

"Yes, you can. It depends. I think rates start at five Cedis and then it depends whether they are hired for one hour or more..." explains Daniel.

I shake my head in disbelief. For the equivalent of about one US dollar and a few cents, I can hire a kayayoo to carry my shopping for me. I suddenly grow silent. Not visible to the eye, I too am carrying a heavy load, but unlike these women head porters, I am carrying it not on my head but in my heart. No wonder it feels so heavy.

The past two months in our new Ghanaian adventure have been the most difficult and trying transition I have faced in a new country. I feel completely lost, confused and bewildered by the corner of the world I find myself in, even though this is my eighth international move, my ninth country to live in, albeit my first time living on the African continent. I thought growing up in a developing country like Pakistan would help me to adjust to life in Ghana, but I now realize it was like expecting a summer spent in Rome to equip you to deal with living anywhere in Europe.

After two months in Ghana, there is still no sight of our container which has been delayed several times, then stuck with customs authorities, then processed incorrectly. As a result, we are starting month number four of living out of suitcases, in hotels, with two kids who still think we are here on a holiday, and keep asking when we will fly back home to Dubai. We are in limbo, having said goodbye to our lives in Dubai but not being able to settle in properly and start our new lives in Ghana. It is starting to take a toll on my mental health. I am tired of being the family cheerleader, keeping everyone else's spirits up while battling my own demons.

For the first time in my long expat life, I feel myself slipping into a depression. What used to be simple everyday tasks feel like massive hurdles at the moment. Grocery shopping in Accra involves going to at least four different supermarkets; one to buy fresh fruit, the other to buy meat, and yet another to buy fish. This is partly the reason behind my visit to Makola Market today, to see if I can buy fresh fruits and vegetables from here, for perhaps half the cost. There is no cheese like Mozzarella to be found in any of the big shops in Accra, so one of the other school moms gives me the number of "this guy who makes fresh mozzarella and delivers it to you if you place an order." Then there is the "guy who delivers fresh eggs of good quality", "the butcher who prepares good lamb chops and lean minced meat" and so on. Trying to do grocery shopping for a family of four can easily take me the whole week to organize! I need to go to two or three ATMs before I can find one that works and accepts my VISA card from Dubai because I still don't have a local bank account, for which I need to show proof of living here through a utility bill and because I still don't have a place to live in – well, it all feels impossible some days.

Settling the kids into two different schools has also been challenging. Six-year-old Mina was visibly nervous walking into her new American school to start first grade in Ghana. Missing her Dubai friends, she *was upset that she didn't get to wear a school uniform like her friends back in Dubai, who were all transitioning to 'big school.' Little battles over which clothes to wear to school in the morning were sometimes a longing for what her life would have been like had we stayed in Dubai. Instead of comforting her, I let her mourn the loss and acknowledged what she had to give up.*

Mikail had to wait four weeks till he could finally start at his new kindergarten. He was ecstatic to start but in his three-year-old head, he still expected to see his classmates and favorite teacher from Dubai at his new school in Accra. "Where is Bassel?" he asked on his first day, inquiring about his best friend from Dubai. I held back tears as I explained once again to him that Bassel was not here, but that there would be tons of new children to make friends with.

Martino was having one of the most stressful starts to a new job, in a new country. He comes back to the hotel one day and announces that his company is facing major cost pressures and accompanied with another organizational restructuring, there are talks underway of shifting their African headquarters from Ghana to South Africa.

"But we just moved here! We haven't even received our container yet! Or unpacked our stuff! Or moved into our house yet. They expect us to move again?" I cry out in complete shock and disbelief.

Martino is angry too. He assures me that nothing will happen immediately. Any decision will be pre-empted by months of planning and could take up to a year. But even that is exhausting knowledge to deal with. I know how quickly a year passes by and I do not want to have to move again next summer. I argue back:

"The kids need stability. And routine. We all do. We just left the UAE and moved to Ghana. You signed a three-year contract. I can't think of moving again so soon!" I conclude helplessly.

In this moment I realize why I am so anxious to get our container. I just want our things to arrive before we are asked to move again. I have never moved to a country and then before we even have a chance to unpack our container, been told to mentally prepare myself for another international move. My mind feels burdened. Each time I meet someone new or make a new friend or discover a great coffee shop in Accra, instead of being excited like I normally would have been, I think to myself, 'what's the point if we have to move again in a year?'

I also realize what going on an adventure truly means.

An adventure is not buying a return ticket for a two-week vacation in Thailand. Knowing that in two weeks' time, you will be back in your familiar surroundings, sitting on your sofa and looking at your holiday photos.

An adventure is when you have no idea how long your time in a new country will last (12 months, 18 months or three years?). There are no return dates or return tickets involved. It means you have no idea what obstacles you will encounter. Or what setbacks you will face. It shows you that nothing is in your control. Simple tasks will feel like huge mountains to conquer. Small things and big things will go wrong. You will be so far out of your comfort zone that you will need to approach your adventure with intention and purpose in order to get through it. You have to live every day to the fullest. You have to take pleasure in the mundane tasks, while retaining your capacity to marvel at the new sights and sounds you experience. You have to enjoy your present surroundings. You have to reach out and make friends along the way. You have to live for today, not for tomorrow.

I snap out of my reverie and turn to Daniel and say, "I wish I could ask her to carry my load, but I'm afraid some things we just have to carry ourselves."

Will our family spirit of adventure see us through this expat posting? Only time will tell.

ADVENTURE MAKES YOUR MOLA FAMILY

Your MOLA Family is now starting to take shape as you add in the various components to your family narrative: your cultures, your languages and your moves.

You started off with a mess. A mess where your different cultures, religions and races in your family make you a multicultural or a cross-cultural family with many faces. Your multicultural family can only flourish once you mix in the different cultural elements in your family and accept the unique blend you create. Your multicultural family is the fabric of your mola, the base upon which you build your global life.

Then you addressed the languages spoken inside your home and outside with your local community. Your bilingual or multilingual family can only flourish when you bring some order to how you communicate with each other and with your environment. Your multilingual family is the thread that helps to stitch your mola and allows you to communicate in your various different languages.

Next you addressed your globally mobile lifestyle and how each country or city you move to adds another layer to your life story and to your family life. Your layers deserve to shine through. Your multi-mobile family is the design on your mola which only appears after you stitch all the different layers together, making the final cuts.

Your MOLA Family may also be a combination of one or two of the above factors. As explained in *Chapter One*, perhaps you are a multicultural family who is also multi-mobile, but monolingual. Perhaps you are a MOLA Family who is multicultural and multilingual, but you are not globally mobile.

The M, O and the L form the 'what' in the making of your MOLA, but the A stands for the 'how.'

The M, O and the L form the 'what' in the making of your MOLA, but the A stands for the 'how.'

After you have mixed your cultures, brought order in your language framework and layered all your international moves and experiences, there is still something missing from your mola. Your shirt has been designed but how do you wear it? With a skirt or with long pants? With matching bottoms or with a scarf?

Similar to a mola, your global life also needs to be 'worn' a certain way, with a certain mindset. You need to ask and ponder over many questions such as:

How do you live your life as a MOLA Family?

How do you combine all the complexities, frustrations, unpredictabilities and the joys you have to embrace as a MOLA Family?

How do you deal with the everyday reality of functioning as a MOLA Family?

How do you not lose sight of the positives in this journey?

What mindset do you need to adopt to ensure you don't sink, but swim?

It is so easy to get caught up in the everyday reality of making your MOLA Family work. But once you have figured out what you need to know, you need to know how to do it. And this is where the last component of your

MOLA toolbox comes in: the A. This chapter focuses on how to pull your MOLA together and the attitude and mindset you need to function as a MOLA Family. The M, O and the L form the basis of your MOLA but without the A your MOLA is incomplete. In order to function as a MOLA Family, the last bit is the most crucial.

DEFINITIONS AND EXAMPLES OF MOLA FAMILIES

MOLA Families are a fusion, and what makes MOLA Families so interesting to dissect is that at any given point in time, they are dealing with some or many of these aspects simultaneously. In real life, you do not deal with challenges related to culture, language and moving in isolation – you deal with them altogether! And if you are not mindful about your mola or the fact that you are a MOLA Family, the mess will creep back in. This is so because with every move new challenges arise. Your kids grow up and their identities are in a constant state of development. Your own identity keeps evolving and how you relate to your partner changes and grows. Constantly exposed to complexities in your intercultural life, your kids' development gets affected too.

MOLA Families are a fusion, and what makes MOLA Families so interesting to dissect is that at any given point in time, they are dealing with some or many of these aspects simultaneously. In real life, you do not deal with challenges related to culture, language and moving in isolation – you deal with them altogether!

All these changes mean your identity evolves as being part of a MOLA Family. It is often not just the external factors that keep on changing (if you used to live in Germany, but now you live in the UK), but your internal compass changes too (perhaps you feel less like an 'other' now due to fewer linguistic barriers). Different members of a MOLA Family can also influence each other's evolution. Your kids may start to influence each other to feel at home in their 'host' country, and you may notice this when you take them back to visit your 'home' country. Three years ago, your MOLA Family may have been rather different than today simply because you face different challenges today.

MEET THE MOLA FAMILIES

A MOLA Family identifies why being out of your comfort zone can bring joy

Jane and her husband are both from the UK. After living in Jersey and the Channel Islands in the UK, they decided to move to Dubai, in the UAE.

"There is a pure joy in choosing to be somewhere and loving that place. Too many of our friends and family appear to be 'stuck' in the UK; they are not willing to take the risk to make a change. We took that risk and we reap the benefits of it every day. We adore the beautiful cultural diversity of the UAE; our daughter, who was born in the UAE in 2013, goes to school here and celebrates Ramadan, Diwali, Christmas, Eid – you name it. Her classmates are from all around the world. We feel blessed to experience this and hope that by opening our minds and hearts (and hers) that the world will become a better, more tolerant, peaceful and loving place," explains Jane.

A MOLA Family identifies why the challenges are worth the opportunities they enjoy

Jo and her husband are both from New Zealand. As a globally mobile family, they have lived in Ireland, Singapore, Hong Kong, China, Cambodia and Japan with their two kids who were born in Singapore and Hong Kong. There have been many challenging moments along their journey and yet as a family they feel lucky.

"There have been plenty of challenges along the way that have evoked strong feelings of anger or floods of tears. My children seeing troops marching past the house in Cambodia with machine guns and bamboo sticks to confront protestors was one such moment I will never forget," notes Jo. And yet Jo recounts the opportunities that they have embraced and enjoyed.

"We have loved creating a network of diverse friends around the world. And the constant reminder of how many truly incredible people there are getting out there and living life by embracing the challenges and opportunities of living outside one's own culture. Our family talks about global politics, political systems and icons; we admire art, religion, language and issues like equality, access to education – and how goddamn lucky we are, as a family. And our kids are only seven and eleven. When our kids ask us questions, it makes us reflect on our own values and assumptions," explains Jo.

A MOLA Family identifies the best thing a global life has given them

Terry Anne and her husband are from Canada. When Terry Anne was 26, she packed her belongings in a backpack and embarked on a six-month trek to Asia. Her subsequent life overseas saw her live in nine countries: Japan, Scotland, the Netherlands, Qatar,

Oman, the United States, Norway, Kazakhstan and India. In the process she raised her three TCK sons, now adults all over the world. After 29 years overseas, she and her husband have recently repatriated to Canada.

"From Roman ruins, to desert sand dunes, to the wonders of India, living globally has given us the opportunity of travel; for adventure, for cultural appreciation and enrichment. Not only has it fostered deep connections and memories in our family, it also gave us the chance to raise global citizens – that's the essence of it really, embracing the diversity of this wondrous world!" explains Terry Anne.

A MOLA Family identifies how adventure can present opportunities for self-growth

Sandra is from Brazil and also a naturalized American citizen. Her husband is an American TCK, raised in Nigeria and Liberia. Together with their children, they have lived their life overseas for more than two decades in various cities in Japan, the United States and Switzerland.

"By being open and adventurous, I got to exercise and eventually master essential skills for a woman living between cultures. I have been able to go through bad days during my international relocations with some joy and certainty because I knew I was learning something of value. Adventure is not hard to experience if you are open to new opportunities, detached from outcomes and perfection. Even though feelings of being uncomfortable are real, they can also be strong motivators and a path to personal development. The adventure then becomes an intersection of challenge and reward," explains Sandra.

A MOLA Family identifies how their sense of adventure has made them adapt

Ginny and her husband are both from the UK. After leading a globally mobile childhood and adulthood, a journey which has seen her live in Sweden, Oman, Bahrain, Nigeria, Indonesia, Egypt, Brazil, Argentina, Australia and Malaysia, Ginny reflects on how her sense of adventure has helped her to adapt to each new experience.

"An expatriate childhood instilled in me a genuine sense of adventure. Environments depicted in films like Born Free (African bush) and Black Stallion (desert island) always seemed in reach. Every decision I have made - university degree, career, partner, have all supported my love of adventure and travel. Knowing that one can face uncertainty and adapt to foreign environments instills a sense of confidence with which to face the next adventure. For me, the key is knowing that one can live a thousand different lives in the same city, and one can always adapt," explains Ginny.

THE CHALLENGES AND OPPORTUNITIES OF BEING A MOLA FAMILY – OUR EXPERTS ADVISE

MOLA Families face many challenges, but it is often their spirit of adventure, optimism, proactivity, flexibility and embracing their new experiences which sustains them in the long run and helps them to see the 'why' in living this complicated, messy life on the move. I collected data from international families through *The Mobile Family Survey* in 2018 through which many MOLA Families shared their experiences. I chose a few examples of the opportunities enjoyed by MOLA families and asked my experts from each field of culture, language and mobility to provide some advice and solutions on how to reap the maximum benefit from those opportunities.

A MOLA Family identifies how adventure has shaped their children

Cynthia was born in Argentina, holds Swedish nationality, and has lived in Sweden, Spain, Saudi Arabia, Yemen and Thailand. Her partner comes from Belgium and together they have lived their married life in Tanzania, Sweden and the Netherlands. Their two children were born in Sweden and together their family enjoys the different ways in which their adventures have shaped their children.

"I read a quote once which said: 'How can you change the world if you've never seen it?' and this rings true for us. We often get questioned about our way of life when it comes to moving the children from one country to another. While I understand how people see it as something negative, that we are depriving our children of stability, I see it as us giving our children a bigger perspective. In a world where so many people build a fence around their house, scared of what is outside, I am proud that my children are curious about the world. Compassionate and tolerant about the differences in people, wanting to understand and learn. And if we can help bring that out not only in them, but also in ourselves, then I am happy," explains Cynthia.

○ ○ ○

Q: HOW CAN PARENTS LIKE CYNTHIA CONTINUE TO RAISE THEIR GLOBALLY MOBILE CHILDREN TO APPRECIATE THE ADVENTURE THEY ARE ALL ON?

A: Expert Ruth Van Reken has some advice for MOLA parents like Cynthia:

Dear Cynthia,

Here are some suggestions for parents like yourself who are raising your children internationally:

- Never forget that growing up cross-culturally changes a child's experience but not the basic need for parental love and support. Don't let your own chaos or stress during a move rob your children of the time and attention they desire.

- Look at each family member before, during and after an international move. If necessary, defer a move until a better time for a child's educational or personal needs. Once you make the transition, remember that each child processes the same event differently. Keep good communication so you can help them navigate the changes successfully.

- Continue having a hopeful, adventuresome, respectful yet realistic attitude. The world is a big place. Why waste an opportunity to explore a new culture and a new land? Encourage your children to learn the local language if it is different from what you speak at home. Take time to visit local historical sites. Don't disparage the local people and cultures. Instead, discuss possible reasons for cultural differences they notice as part of helping your children develop the gift of lifelong cross-cultural awareness and skills.

- Have and maintain core values as a family, as a way to introduce stability. What are the negotiables and non-negotiables by which you live? Portable traditions, keeping religious holidays, modeling respect, etc., are all part of establishing a family identity that transcends the borders of each move.

- Expect to enjoy the journey! Ultimately, it is a rich heritage when done well!

Best,
Ruth

"Never forget that growing up cross-culturally changes a child's experience but not the basic need for parental love and support. Don't let you own chaos or stress during a move rob your children of the time and attention they desire."
—Ruth Van Reken.

A MOLA Family identifies their opportunities in embracing two different cultures to create their own family culture

Rachael is from the United States, while her husband is from Palestine but also holds an American passport. Together they have lived in the US, Palestine and the UAE, and their twins were born in 2016 in the US. They currently live in Abu Dhabi.

"It's challenging with the different cultures sometimes. As Americans, we are more laid back and open. In a Middle Eastern culture, things are often kept more private and handled between family. Also, relationships between men and women are handled completely differently. How my husband and I met and dated before marriage is not how a typical Middle Eastern relationship is. And also, not the way we will teach our children, which is a total double standard but that's how it most likely will be," explains Rachael.

∘ ∘ ∘

Q: HOW CAN MOLA FAMILIES LIKE RACHAEL EMBRACE THEIR DIFFERENT CULTURES WITH A SENSE OF OPENNESS AND ADVENTURE?

A: Expert Sundae Schneider-Bean has some advice on culture and creativity for Rachael:

Dear Rachael,

Keep in mind that raising multicultural children abroad is a dynamic and ongoing intercultural interaction. I recommend the following techniques to parents like you:

- Rather than 'my way', 'my partner's way', or 'the local way', embrace a constant negotiation of 'our way' and what that means.
- Pay attention to what is emerging for each member of the family as important in "our way."
- Use this co-creation of your family's third culture as an opportunity to incorporate the best of all worlds.

Since your children will learn from the attitudes and behaviors that you model, it is equally important for parents to build their own intercultural competencies. Develop your own intercultural competencies and embrace the ongoing opportunity to negotiate a third culture to most optimally co-lead your multicultural family abroad.

Here is how you can further develop your intercultural competencies:

- Resist the temptation to simplify 'culture' to 'nation.' Notice when you use nationality as a justification to over-generalize stereotypes to large groups of people.

- Explore your own cultural preferences and tendencies and encourage your partner to do the same so that you understand how these impact your relationship and parenting approach.

- Learn the dimensions of cultural values (e.g. relationship vs task orientation) and how they function so that you can more neutrally identify similarities and differences across cultures and understand better why people behave as they do.

Best,
Sundae

"Rather than 'my way', 'my partner's way', or 'the local way', embrace a constant negotiation of 'our way' and what that means."
— Sundae Schneider-Bean

A MOLA Family talks about the joys of being multilingual

Chontelle was born in Australia, she is half-Italian and her native language is English. Her husband was born in Italy and his first language is Italian. Together, they have learned some French and Spanish along the way and each other's native languages of English and Italian. As a family with young kids they have lived together in Italy and have just moved to Australia.

"I love that my children have learned new languages and are growing up to be multilingual. I believe languages open children up to great advantages in life. Not just communication advantages but also the outlook they have on life. I see they are more open-minded, and curious about different people and cultures, and especially people who speak different languages; they have a thirst for learning about it all," explains Chontelle.

○ ○ ○

Q: HOW CAN MOLA FAMILIES LIKE CHONTELLE'S USE THEIR DIFFERENT LANGUAGES TO ENJOY THE ADVENTURE THEY ARE ON?

A: Expert Rita Rosenback has some advice for MOLA parents like Chontelle's to enjoy their family's multilingual journey and celebrate the small successes along the way:

Dear Chontelle,

As parents of children who we are raising to speak two, three or even more languages, we should from time to time stop and take stock of what we *have* achieved. It is so easy to beat yourself up for not having read, played or Skyped enough, arranged those visits and looked for playgroups or camps in the right language. The list of what we tend to see as failures is endless. However, all parents do the best they can for their children at any given point, in the circumstances they are in, with the knowledge they have, and the energy they can muster.

If you have managed to pass on enough language skills so your children can follow a conversation in a language – that is a big thing! You have given them something that can be built upon and enables them to create and maintain more relationships. If your children can make themselves understood in an additional language thanks to you – well done! You have achieved more than many trained language teachers do. If your kids grow up fluent in more than one language, I take my hat off to you! You should be so proud. You have given them a gift for life. A gift that keeps giving across generations, even when you are no longer here.

Best,
Rita

"If your kids grow up fluent in more than one language, I take my hat off to you! You should be so proud. You have given them a gift for life."
— Rita Rosenback.

YOUR MOLA TOOLBOX:
A IS FOR ADVENTURE

In my 17 years as an expat, I have never seen anything like it before. As we pull onto the side of a dirt road, half an hour outside the Ghanaian port city of Tema, it comes into full view. There it is: our 40-foot container – broken down in the middle of nowhere. Each box inside of it is a piece of our life story. I take a big gulp and step outside to see the operations team of 15 people who are trying to explore various options of airlifting the container, removing it, replacing the truck or figuring out another solution. The "last resort" option is to open up our container in the middle of this busy road in West Africa and transfer its contents to three to four smaller trucks.

It has already been stuck here for three days and still there is no progress. Over the past few days, we have been forced to move into a second hotel which has been even more disruptive for our family and routine and for our kids' sense of stability. Martino has not been able to focus on his work and has spent two days meeting and talking to various stakeholders, trying to sort out this mess. Amidst all this chaos, I have not been able to send the kids to school today because it seemed logistically impossible. We are exhausted and want to see an end to this ordeal.

Our attractive expat package did not include the toll this move has taken on our nerves, on our mental health and on our marriage. Martino and I have fought daily, upset at the lack of progress and frustrated at the lack of control we have over the situation.

Now he turns to me, gives my hands a big squeeze and says, "I promise we'll figure this out today."

I watch him take charge. After a few hours a decision is reached. The "last resort option" is the only option left. It is risky, it is dangerous. Our container could slide down and go rolling in the ditch when they try to unhook it from the truck. There is a risk of damage involved and a question mark over how much insurance would cover. The operations team weighs all the pros and cons and advises that we open up the container.

With our hearts in our mouths, we agree.

I watch as a team of men bring a long wrench to open the lock on the container while the others carry forth metal slides to attach to the end, to allow for access to the boxes inside. Suddenly, a huge gust of wind sweeps us and when I look again, the container is still standing, and its doors are open. Nothing has moved.

Martino and I wrap our arms tightly around each other. Our sighs of relief are audible. So are everyone else's. The transfer begins. It has to be orchestrated slowly in order to avoid any damage in the process. After five hours, four trucks are loaded and dispatched to our new house in Accra. The Chief Operating Officer overseeing this operation turns to us and says, "It's quite the start to your African adventure!"

I don't know whether to laugh or cry, so I do both. Through the tears of relief, a sudden realization hits me.

When the going gets tough, your MOLA comes to your rescue. It determines whether you give up or soldier on.

In this very moment I realize for the first time that my MOLA tools allow me to look at a disaster, tap into my reserves of resilience and not lose hope, even when things feel hopeless. While others may fall apart, I don't, even though I feel like I have come close to it. I draw strength from knowing that as awful and unnerving as this experience is to go through, one day I will write about it and turn it into an oft-told story at the dining table. I cannot control the situation, but I can control my attitude and reaction to the situation and the only way to do this is to put my hands up in the air and accept that adventures never go according to plan.

In my framework of a MOLA Family, A definitely stands for adventure. Without it, your MOLA is incomplete and unfinished. Adventure is the attitude that binds your MOLA together. It helps you appreciate the positive experiences and gets you through the challenging experiences.

It helps you to embrace everything that happens to you - good, bad, ugly, big and small - and include it in your life story. It helps you not to give up on a bad day. It helps you truly enjoy a good day. It helps you to appreciate this journey you are on and to accept it with grace and humility. It teaches you how to be resilient, even when things don't go your way.

Adventure is the attitude that binds your MOLA together. It helps you appreciate the positive experiences and gets you through the challenging experiences.

ADVENTURE WILL KEEP YOUR MOLA FAMILY FRESH AND NEW

Why is adventure so crucial to your MOLA Family? I think adventure is what keeps your mola feeling fresh and new. It's the part that will constantly change and allows you to change with it.

Adventure will help you keep a sense of curiosity, because being a MOLA Family means you constantly discover new things about yourself, your partner, your children and your family as a whole. For instance, I discovered that even though I had grown up in a developing country like Pakistan and was more familiar with things not working, people not showing up when they said they would and having lots of household help around - these aspects still continued to bother me, because I let them. I found myself getting so worked up about the inefficient process of getting a local phone number and SIM card, that I almost left the

Vodafone shop in Accra Mall. Martino, on the other hand, who had grown up in Germany in a culture where order, reliability and punctuality were key pillars of society, had an easier time dealing with it all. His attitude was: "This is an adventure, I can't control it, so I won't let it bother me." It meant his way of approaching our expat life in Ghana was a lot healthier and often when he saw me getting worked up about something inconsequential, he'd just say, "Hey, it's part of the adventure!"

Adventure also means you can appreciate and enjoy the positive experiences more consciously. Learning a new language, learning new customs, trying out new food for the first time are all enhanced when we view these as learning experiences that we can add to our MOLA. We have loved trying Ghanaian cuisine since our move to West Africa. We have signed up for a host of various activities – from chocolate and cocoa tasting to West African drumming and music classes. Day trips and excursions with the kids to other regions of Ghana are helping us to keep that spirit of adventure alive while exploring more of the country we find ourselves in.

Adventure means you will always be in for a surprise, no matter how well you understand your MOLA Family, because you can never predict everything. I had not realized what a creature of habit our son Mikail really was, until our move to Ghana. Routine, structure and consistent habits were what he needed to thrive in a new environment. This meant giving him the same snack and lunchbox every day and sticking to our routine of being dropped to school by Papa and being picked up by Mama. I realized sticking to routines made it easier to parent my toddler, so when it came to him I kept things as simple as possible.

Adventure also means that you need to trust and have faith in your MOLA Family and not let setbacks or misunderstandings question your whole family setup or way of life. There is no doubt that you will face challenges and setbacks. Maybe one of your children becomes fluent in your native tongue while the other one doesn't, even though you are not parenting them differently. Have trust in your MOLA Family and try to figure out what the underlying problem could be before you question your entire family setup or linguistic framework.

Adventure will ensure that you can let go of the notion that your MOLA will ever be finished; it is an ever evolving and developing concept, with the journey itself being the goal or destination. It means that all the different cultural, linguistic and mobility influences will continuously fuse into an ever-changing, adventurous cocktail. After 12 years of marriage, in which we have lived in five countries together, I thought we had figured it all out. The truth is that our MOLA keeps evolving and challenges will keep creeping up.

Adventure means that you become more resilient in the face of adversity. The more resilient you become, the more things you will perceive as an adventure rather than a disaster. MOLA Families become great at bouncing back and have a high level of bouncebackability. They understand that the reason they bounce back is because they are okay with not being perfect.

Adventure means that you become more resilient in the face of adversity. The more resilient you become, the more things you will perceive as an adventure rather than a disaster.

A MOLA helps you to see that you can never 'perfect' living this messy life, but that you can help develop the toolbox that you need to live this life. The toolbox every MOLA Family can remember, and practice daily is:

M: Mix

O: Order

L: Layer

A: Adventure

These are the tools to help you navigate your messy international life. Just like a Guna woman making a mola chooses a fabric, selects her threads, and takes out a pair of fine scissors before she starts sewing, layering and making her final design, MOLA Families need to **mix** their different cultures, races and religions together, sew in some **order** with their languages to raise their bilingual/multilingual kids, **layer** all their moves and life experience in different countries together, and then embrace their life with a sense and attitude of **adventure**.

THE FIVE RULES FOR MOLA FAMILIES

1. BUILD UP YOUR CULTURAL INTELLIGENCE (CQ)

MOLA Families need to do the work that is needed to enjoy the global life and the different cultures they share and experience. One way to do this is for MOLA Families to start by building their Cultural Intelligence (CQ). Interculturalist Trisha Carter explains:

"There are four parts to CQ: Drive, Knowledge, Strategy, Action. Some ways to build them are:

○ CQ Drive: As parents, be clear on your family story and your 'why' for the value you place on multicultural experiences and share these often with your children. How you met, where the children were born and have lived, great experiences you have had are all part of that story.

- CQ Knowledge: What do you know about the place you are living in? Its history, geography, music, sports and sports stars, movies and movie stars. Have a competition as a family to learn new things about the country or culture and share them together.

- CQ Strategy: Encourage your children to notice how people interact in this location. From the volume people speak, to the handshakes or kisses as greetings, to the games children are playing – taking notice is a great skill to develop. Use journaling to observe and reflect.

- CQ Action: Practice a new language together or non-verbal skills and encourage each other to use the skills."

2. KNOW YOUR CORE VALUES

It is vital for MOLA Families to sit down just like most big corporations do and chart out their core values. Jerry Jones advises parents that in order to function as a MOLA Family: "Know your core values. Get crystal clear on what you want your kids to learn, know and experience in regard to their birth and their host cultures. Also consider how you want them to connect to your own passport culture. Let your kid dictate their own story. It's their story not yours. If people ask them invasive questions about their ethnicity and why they don't look like you, give them the option to respond as they feel comfortable. Help them build that story with appropriate guidance but let them have the final say. Protect their freedom to change over time and never insist that they resonate most with your favorite part."

3. FIND FAMILIARITY IN THE UNKNOWN

MOLA Families often find themselves out of their comfort zones. Being able to find familiarity in the unknown is a great way to bridge cultures and help you find common ground. I realized, with glee, that shopping for clothes in Ghana reminded me of how we used to shop in Pakistan when I was growing up there. There were no department stores back then, only bazaars full of colorful fabrics. In Accra, there is also a similar concept of buying unstitched fabric, choosing how many yards or meters you require to make a skirt out of colorful 'kente' cloth, designing your own clothes and then giving it to the tailor to stitch. Finding this little common ground between two very different cultures brought joy and helped me find a sense of home in a new corner of the world.

4. WEAR YOUR MOLA PROUDLY

Just as the Guna women in Panama and Colombia take great pride in wearing their mola shirts, MOLA Families too should proudly wear their MOLA identities. A mola is something you wear and show to the world. It is something you are comfortable wearing which conveys a certain image or identity to the world. It is important for MOLA Families to proudly display their MOLA and Chapter Six discusses how to do this in detail.

5. DON'T TAKE YOUR MOLA FOR GRANTED

Making a MOLA is hard work, so don't take your MOLA Family for granted. If you don't put in the work required to make it function, you might face problems. Constant communication is required. Reinvent your family culture with each move; it is okay to add in new traditions or routines based on your current surroundings. Strive to consciously keep your MOLA alive, as it keeps on changing over time. Don't allow the mess to creep back in. If you feel your international life getting messy again, revisit your MOLA. (What element of the local culture can you mix in? Where do you need more order in your family life? Are you hiding your layers in order to fit in? Are you approaching your daily obstacles and challenges with an adventurous attitude?)

CHAPTER SUMMARY

1. Your MOLA Family is starting to take shape. You have added in your cultures (the fabric of your mola), your languages (the thread of your mola) and your moves (the design of your mola). Keep in mind though, that your MOLA is ever-changing and constantly developing.

2. In order to function as a MOLA Family, you need to create your own unique family culture by embracing all aspects of your life story in a healthy and transparent way.

3. In your MOLA toolbox, A stands for adventure. In creating a MOLA Family, it is important to adopt a sense of adventure in enjoying the challenges and opportunities that you face on a daily basis. Adventure allows you to enjoy your MOLA and all the experiences you encounter in your mobile life.

4. Your MOLA toolbox is now complete. M: mix, O: order, L: layer, and A: adventure. This is the recipe for going from a mess to MOLA!

5. To enjoy the adventure in your MOLA Family, it is important to develop your Cultural Intelligence (CQ), know your core family values, find familiarity and joy in the unknown, wear your MOLA proudly and never take your MOLA for granted.

ACTIVITY: WHAT DOES YOUR MOLA FAMILY LOOK LIKE?

What would your MOLA Family look like? You can be as creative as you like and come up with ideas that fit your family the best. A mola is your personal blueprint, so no one can prescribe what would go on your mola, but I am here to help you to start thinking and visualizing your mola, as a fun exercise to do with your family.

Your MOLA Family could consist of:

- Colors
- Fabric
- Monuments/buildings
- Symbols
- Shapes
- Flowers
- Animals/birds
- Landscapes
- Emotions
- Sensations
- Experiences

Jot down a few things in each category to see what you come up with

Come up with an icon for each and draw your own

Think about the places you have lived in or the cultures you belong to. Think about what food has shaped your family life or which shapes your family identifies with. Perhaps you have lived in France and want the Eiffel Tower to be one of your icons on your MOLA. Imagine how you would represent your family life if you were to design your own shirt.

Go to my website www.andthenwemovedto.com to download a blank shirt and start drawing your mola.

In the meantime, for some inspiration, here is our mola:

Our MOLA Family would consist of:

- **Color:** Bright turquoise, blue and white to signify the image of peering out of an airplane and seeing turquoise water below and blue skies and white clouds above.
- **Fabric:** The fabric for my mola is chiffon – a sheer appearance, lightweight, a magical luster both slippery, yet graceful. I chose a slippery fabric like chiffon because it has been a slippery slope creating our MOLA Family and slips still always happen. I have to carefully catch and drape the fabric to make it work, just like I have to constantly navigate new challenges in our MOLA Family. Like most other crepe fabrics, chiffon can be difficult to work with because of its sheer and fine texture. In fact, chiffon often needs a thicker lining underneath to support it, because on its own it is versatile yet weak. As a MOLA Family, we are constantly ensuring that we have that solid and secure foundation underneath in terms of who we are, to enable us to drape that beautiful chiffon fabric gracefully over it.
- **Monuments/buildings:** Brandenburg Gate (Germany), The Quaid's Mazaar (Pakistan).

- **Symbols:** Flags from all the different countries we have lived in or tiny letter M's because all our names in the family start with an 'M.'
- **Shapes:** Triangles (because we have three dominant cultures at home which are always at interplay).
- **Flowers:** Orchid (national flower of Singapore where our daughter Mina was born).
- **Animals/birds:** Falcon (national symbol of the UAE where our son Mikail was born).
- **Landscapes:** The desert, and the sea, olive fields.

Figure 6: An illustration of my mola by artist Helena Jalanka.

CONVERSATION STARTERS

Here are a few conversation starters for you and your family to answer, perhaps over a weekend family dinner:

1. **As a MOLA Family, you have a distinct family culture you create and live by.**

   - Finish the sentence: "We are a family who…" It might be something you all love to do, or something you celebrate, or something about your beliefs.

2. **Adventure is both an attitude and an actual experience. It is both tangible and intangible.**

   - How do you keep the spirit and sense of adventure alive in your MOLA Family?

3. **MOLA Families are a fusion of cultures, languages, nationalities, experiences and identities. I often compare my MOLA Family to a marble cake with chocolate and vanilla swirls and patterns all mixed in together, in an unpredictable design.**

   - How would you best describe your MOLA Family fusion? Play-Doh: when you mix the colors together, you can't unmix or separate them? A pomegranate: rich with gems on the inside, but dull and plain from the outside? A chameleon: who constantly changes color depending on its surroundings? Or something else?

CHAPTER SIX

SHOWING YOUR MOLA TO THE WORLD

"Your mola, unique and complex in its layering of events, emotions and experiences, in what is folded back and what remains covered, in what is well stitched and what may need mending, is who you are. Hide it and you have little to show. Display its richness, add to it, share it – and you may change your life and your world."

Norma M. McCaig

SHOWING MY MOLA

The anticipation builds up as we exit Wolfsburg and start driving down the Autobahn in the direction of Hannover. The roads are icy and every few minutes there are signs flashing in German "Langsam fahren" (drive carefully). As we approach the quaint village of Delligsen, the German countryside looks like something out of a fairytale. Probably because it is. Legend has it that the Brothers Grimm based their popular children's story of Snow White here and that the seven dwarfs came from the seven hills in this idyllic part of the countryside – where the gentle, rolling hills dominate the landscape. This area looks beautiful in the summertime, but today it is a cold and rainy December in the state of Niedersachsen (Lower Saxony) and we are home for Christmas.

I am freezing and the only one sitting with my winter coat on inside the car. As I look out the window of my father-in-law's Volkswagen, I think about how holidays and special occasions require extra negotiation, patience and understanding from all the different parts of our family. Like most family holidays, time spent with our extended family is precious, although an exhausting balance of mish-mashed cultures, food, languages, traditions and expectations.

"We have Christmas presents for Mina and Mikail, and also for you and Martino!" say our extended Italian and German family members.

"Don't worry, I didn't use any white wine in making this sauce for the pasta!" calls out my mother-in-law from her sister's kitchen.

"Did you get the day off to celebrate Christmas in Pakistan?" asks my German sister-in-law in German.

"Mama, I know we celebrate both Christmas and Eid, but my favorite holiday is still Chinese New Year!" declares Mina excitedly.

"How do I say the words 'political instability' in German?" I ask Martino in the middle of a heated discussion on politics and why it is so hard for democracy to take root in many developing countries.

"Don't worry there's no pork on the menu today!" says our aunt in charge of cooking Christmas lunch.

"What is Christmas like in Dubai?" asks our half-German, half-Italian cousin as he offers me a non-alcoholic drink.

"As per the Italian tradition of my husband's hometown of Basilicata, I've made sweet pasta for the first course," says our German aunt, who honors her husband's family tradition each year at Christmas. Pasta made sweet, to signify a sweet occasion.

"Do you guys know where you are moving to next? Which continent is left: Africa? South America?" asks one of our Italian uncles.

I force myself to slow down. My brain is hearing the chatter in two languages, which I'm translating in my head into my own two languages. Each time I turn to speak to someone it is in a different language – Urdu with the kids, English with Martino, German with everyone else and a few words of small talk in Italian, especially when it comes to praising the food. Sometimes, the same joke is repeated in three or four languages around the table, till everyone gets it.

We all laugh each time.

Soon, it is time to sit down and enjoy the food. After 12 years of being married into Martino's family, I know now to pace myself for their family Christmas lunch, prepared by his German aunt, based on tradition but modified for current family requirements including four picky kids. There are usually around five courses;

Antipasto (an appetizer)

Primo piatto (sweet pasta)

Secondo piatto (savory pasta)

Hauptgericht (meat, vegetables and salads)

Nachtisch (dessert, fruits and coffee)

Just as the languages keep switching, so does the food. The menu starts off Italian and then turns German, without any explanations. One minute we are eating food from the south of Italy, the next we are eating food from the north of Germany. I tug at my black dress (a present from my mother-in-law) wishing there was more room as the food coma takes over. There are lulls in the conversation, and that's when I look around the room and feel the sense of warmth radiating across the table.

In this family, full of immigrants, expats, cross-cultural kids, multilingual parents and multicultural grandparents, it is okay to show your mola. We all show our mola proudly. Our mola is our way of holding our story and sharing it proudly for the world to see.

SHOWING YOUR MOLA

Chapter Four and *Chapter Five* discussed the importance of 'showing' your mola. Why is it so important to show your mola?

"Story is the medium we humans have used for thousands of years to create, convey and recall meaning in our lives," explains Doug Ota, author of the book *Safe Passage: How mobility affects people and what international schools should do about it*. He highlights the importance of "holding the story" as a crucial skill that high-mobility people must learn how to do.

"The visible wear of a mola indicates its authenticity," explains Tyler Jackson in his online article 'What is a Mola?' By wearing and showing your mola and being proud of your MOLA Family, you are acknowledging and accepting your life story. You are embracing the different cultures, races and religions that may make up your multicultural family. You are proud of the different languages you and your family use to communicate. And you are taking ownership of how your globally mobile lifestyle has changed you and shaped you and your family's identities. MOLA Families need to take inspiration from the Guna women in Panama and Colombia, who are stitching a mola to wear. Wearing it shows they are comfortable expressing who they are. For many MOLA Families, the concept is the same.

By showing your mola and being proud of your MOLA Family, you are acknowledging and accepting your life story.

Think of your mola as a coat of arms; representative of who you are, where you come from, where you identify with the most and so on. It is your individual seal. One you will be proud to see by your family name. Just as Meghan Markle's coat of arms included blue to represent the Pacific Ocean and golden poppies from her native California, so should your mola represent who you are as a family.

A mola is thus a healthy metaphor for the metaphor of your international lives. 'Showing' your mola therefore could mean several different things. For example:

- When asked the ubiquitous "Where are you from?" question you could reply "We are a MOLA Family" before explaining what a mola is and highlighting your multicultural roots, the different languages you speak or the different people and places that feel like home to you.

- It means being comfortable in sharing the fact that you have multiple identities in your family.

- It means acknowledging that although you may be different from many people in the room, you can still relate to them based partly on a common interest, a common language or a common place you both lived in.

- It means accepting that your family is diverse, and although you may never fit in one society completely, you may fit in several societies to different degrees.

- It means that instead of only celebrating the customs, traditions and holidays of your home country (or countries) or the customs, tradition and holidays of your host country, you will celebrate a mix of both as you create your own unique blend of family cultures.

- It means that you speak your native languages proudly with your kids and explain to friends, neighbors, teachers, school and so on, that you are raising your children bilingually or multilingually.

- It means you accept and make allowances for other people's religious beliefs and rules too.

- It means you practice 'linguistic empathy'; you believe every family has the right to raise their kids in the languages of their choice. You respect their choice. You do not make fun of other people's accents, vocabulary or any mistakes they may make while speaking in a language that is not their mother tongue.

- It means you travel with your family to continue to expose them to different cultures, languages and societies to enrich their understanding and appreciation of the world.

Showing your mola can thus mean different things depending on who you are showing it to and the particular circumstances. At its core, remains the idea that you and your family are unique, and showing your 'true colors' helps you engage with the world in a more positive and fruitful way.

THE CHALLENGES AND OPPORTUNITIES OF SHOWING YOUR MOLA TO OTHERS

Showing your mola often brings forth its own unique challenges and opportunities. I collected data from hundreds of international families through *The Mobile Family Survey* in 2018, through which participants shared their experiences from around the world.

A MOLA Family identifies how choosing a school for their kids is a tough decision

Hanna is from Hungary, while her husband is from South Africa. Before her marriage Hanna lived in Hungary, the US, Austria and Germany, while as a family they have lived in the UAE, where her two children were born in 2010 and 2012. Hanna explains one of her biggest challenges is trying to figure out where home is for her family and where they see themselves creating a future. This decision makes choosing a school system that will provide continuity for their children a real challenge in a place like Dubai.

"Our biggest challenge in the UAE is which school system should I select for my kids who are not from the UK, USA or France: German or Arabic?" asks Hanna.

A MOLA Family shows the difficulty of their family back home not understanding their TCKs

Matt and his wife are both from the United States. Their mobile life has taken them to Canada and Spain. They are busy raising their two TCKs who are able to adopt a European mindset and hold this perspective as well as enjoy an American outlook. Matt identifies that he appreciates how his family is able to learn and experience the world in different ways, but that this also poses certain challenges.

"Raising TCKs far from family is difficult. We struggle with our family not understanding the uniqueness of TCKs and their sense of belonging in their current country," explains Matt.

A MOLA Family identifies how raising kids away from extended family is challenging

Marissa is from Spain, while her husband is from Australia. Marissa has lived in Spain, the UK, US, UAE, Jordan and Egypt, but together with her husband they have been settled in Dubai, which is also where their two children were born. Marissa loves the fact that due to their international upbringing, her kids are able to enjoy a global outlook and experience so many different cultures first hand. But she also acknowledges that living abroad means missing out on support from extended family.

"We struggle with not being able to enjoy the support of our families in our everyday lives, and it not being possible for them to participate in our celebrations such as birthdays, events and successes at school," explains Marissa.

A MOLA Family identifies how a life abroad has accentuated differences with their extended families

Divya and her husband are both from India. Before her marriage Divya lived in Malaysia, Nigeria, India and the UK, while as a couple she and her husband have lived in India, the UK, the UAE and South Africa. Their teenage daughter was born in Jaipur. Divya explains that as a result of living and viewing the world as a whole, her daughter has adopted an expanded world view.

"However, one of my biggest challenges is the mismatch in thinking between us (as the "well-traveled family") and the rest of the family. Parts of our family cannot understand why we like to keep things personal and quiet and why we don't share everything," explains Divya.

A MOLA Family identifies how lack of spousal employment causes gender inequality in their family roles

Helena is from Sweden, while her husband is from Canada. As a couple they have lived in Albania, Kenya, Slovakia, Palestine, the US and Sweden. Helena mentions that they love the fact that their life abroad means they spend less money and time on things and property and as a result their global lives have made them less materialistic. However, this lifestyle does not come without its fair share of challenges.

"Spousal employment is the biggest continued challenge I face. Dependence on the working spouse for income, health insurance, future pension etc. brings with it gender inequality and self-confidence issues," explains Helena.

A MOLA Family identifies how hard it is to make decisions regarding "where to settle"

Mandy and her husband are both from the UK. Their globally mobile life has taken them from England to Bahrain to the UAE. After more than a decade of living in the Middle East, Mandy shares both the opportunities and the challenges that her family of five faces.

"Where will my children call home after their full-time education? And where shall we settle in retirement? My children love going to our home country for holidays. They see it as their home. As a parent, I've made my home where my family is, and I don't share their feelings. I think we've given them privileges and experiences they would have missed out on growing up in the same town or country their whole lives. But the children see how their cousins live back in England and wish for the same freedom. I'm hoping when they're grown up with families of their own, hopefully in another country of their choice, they'll look back and realize why we chose to bring them up in a different culture," explains Mandy.

SPECIAL SITUATIONS

Many MOLA Families living around the world also face special challenges, such as divorce, death or a split family where quite often one partner is working abroad while the other partner stays in their home country (or a different country) with the children. This last scenario is in fact becoming increasingly common in many globally mobile families and was also brought up through *The Mobile Family Survey* 2018.

MOLA Families thus may face challenges such as single parenting in a new or foreign culture, going through a divorce in a country where they may not have equal rights, and living at a distance from their spouse which poses its own set of problems in terms of family life and culture. Katia Vlachos, an expat transition coach and author of the book *A Great Move* explains why expat divorce is hard:

"Expats experience the usual challenges of divorce more intensely, mainly because the support system they would have had at home isn't there. Legal and jurisdictional questions also can be much more complex when you live in another country. Other practical difficulties with expat divorce include what happens to residence and work permits after the breakup," says Katia.

SHOWING YOUR MOLA TO SCHOOLS

One of the most important places to 'show' your mola is to the school or schools that your children attend. When living a globally mobile lifestyle, choosing the 'right' school for your international kids is a process many international families struggle with. Different academic curriculums, different methodologies, new ways of learning, changing the language of instruction, making friends, extra-curricular activities offered, and the diversity of both teachers and the student body are aspects that figure prominently in a school search. Mobile families also search for schools that will provide the greatest chance of continuity in academic system for their children.

Settling into a new school can be a challenging process for international children as they have to start from scratch and build familiar routines, be comfortable in their new environment and start to feel safe and accepted by their peers and teachers.

Kate Berger is a child and adolescent psychologist and founder of The Expat Kids Club, who counsels young expats and their families. In one of her articles written for the *Financial Times,* she recommends that parents ask the following questions from prospective schools in order to make sure they pick the right one for their child:

1. How large is the school's expat population?
2. Does the school have a buddy or ambassador program?
3. Does the school involve families in supporting expat students?
4. Is the school willing to exchange information with the child's previous school?
5. Does the school staff include caring adults who are knowledgeable about expat transitions and are on call to meet the child?

These questions are a great starting point, because they help you understand a school and its culture better, specifically in the context of transition.

In addition to this, it is important to actively 'show' your mola to help you make the choice that is the 'right fit' for your MOLA Family.

How can you 'show' your mola to schools you are interested in and later to the school that you choose for your child?

SHOW YOUR MOLA WHEN CHOOSING A SCHOOL

- Take a school tour or join an information session and mention specifically if you are raising a bilingual or a multilingual kid and the languages that your child speaks or is fluent in. If you are Dutch and your partner is Turkish, and you have raised your child in Luxembourg, then your child may struggle initially to adapt to an English-speaking school in Dubai. This is normal, but as a parent it is important to mention your child's multilingual background and literacy as an advantage and try to gauge the level of language support a particular school is willing to give to work together to overcome any challenges in learning that may arise because of language. As a MOLA Family, you may also decide to choose a school offering bilingual education over a school which has a weak or non-existent language program.

- Is the curriculum that the school follows compatible with your globally mobile lifestyle? While a Primary Years Programme (PYP) may be a common international based curriculum, the Australian National Curriculum may limit your future choices for education in a different corner of the world. Show your mola by asking questions and assessing a current school and its curriculum based on the assumption of moving again – it should fit your child's current educational needs and allow you a way to continue your child's future academic needs in quite possibly a different country. How would credits transfer from one system to another? Continuity in academic systems is a crucial point to consider.

- If you and your partner are from different countries, and you do not have a clear-cut preference for one school system or the other, then try to visit different schools to get a better idea. Many British families living overseas for example, opt for a GCSE curriculum because that may be what they are familiar with, or there is the expectation that their child will return to the UK for higher education. But if you are a multicultural family with no clear home base to repatriate to, then choosing a school becomes tricky and confusing. Explain your MOLA background to the school Principal or Head of Admissions; are you expecting to move again in a few years or are you looking to consolidate and have some stability and continuity over the next few years in terms of your children's education?

SHOW YOUR MOLA ONCE YOUR CHILD IS AT SCHOOL

- Highlight your child's diverse background. This could include your multicultural family, or your child's international upbringing in various corners of the world.

- Ask your child's teacher if they can do a show and tell for international day instead of dressing up in one costume, because it is often difficult for kids who come from a MOLA Family to choose just one.

- Ask your child's teacher to help your child express their identity or sense of home. Give them more than one option when you ask them to do an assignment on your 'home country.' Allow them the flexibility to choose a 'home country' that they feel they are from, even if that is different from their nationality (or nationalities) on paper.

- Is your child learning either the country's local language or a foreign language at school? Encourage your child to learn the local language, local customs and culture which can be a great way for a child from a MOLA Family to feel comfortable and familiar in their new surroundings and form healthy attachments to a place.

In his book *Safe Passage: How mobility affects people and what international schools can do about it,* Doug Ota explains that if handled properly, mobility can be a catalyst for growth. International schools can play a big role in creating a safe harbor to help children through a transition, and so can MOLA Families.

SHOWING YOUR MOLA TO INTERNATIONAL COMPANIES/ ORGANIZATIONS

Many families are sent abroad by either big multinational companies like Shell, Nestlé or Procter & Gamble or international organizations such as the United Nations. Diplomats are posted abroad by their governments and missionaries and NGOs also send families abroad on specific assignments.

Regardless of whether you are an expat, a diplomat, a military officer or a missionary – it is important to 'show' your mola to the company/ organization/entity who sends you abroad. The reason is quite simple. By showing your mola, you will increase the chances and likelihood of success for your international assignment. By attending to your family needs and making sure your sponsor is aware of your challenges, you will reduce the risk of an expatriation cut short. International assignments are already difficult for the individual, but for a family they can be harder. While relocating the entire family provides countless opportunities and fantastic experiences, it is a difficult process and not without risks.

By showing your mola, you will increase the chances and likelihood of success for your international assignment. By attending to your family needs and making sure your sponsor is aware of your challenges, you will reduce the risk of an expatriation cut short.

Not surprisingly, expatriate failure statistics show that family issues are a major cause of failed assignments, where the employee's partner and children may encounter difficulty adjusting to the new country. A 2014 survey by Cartus found that 70% of assignees will have their partner accompany them, and almost half will have dependent children. Many of these issues could be alleviated by "research of all components of relocation for a long-term assignment, especially those factors that affect spouses, partners and dependents."

So how best can MOLA Families show their mola to the organizations that send them abroad?

- **Share your family complexity:** Schedule a pre-move meeting with your organization/HR department to specifically discuss the complexity of your family culture, nationalities and needs. For example, instead of registering with just one embassy in your host country, you might need to register at three. Instead of filing tax returns in just one country, you might need to do it in two countries. To send a family of four (each with different nationalities) will require more paperwork and coordination in order to obtain the relevant visas and permits. If your kids are adopted, check to make sure you are their legal guardian in the country you are moving to. If you are in a same-sex marriage, and are being posted to the Middle East, ask how this will impact your family, if your marriage is not recognized in a country like Kuwait. If you are Muslim, but your partner is Christian, do you require legal assistance to set up your wills under Shariah law in the United Arab Emirates? If you are a Hindu-Muslim couple being posted to Dubai and plan to give birth to your first child there, will you have any difficulty in having your marriage recognized and obtaining a birth certificate for your child under UAE local law? MOLA Families deal with incredible complexities depending on where they live, so discuss any questions or concerns you may have on logistical or bureaucratic processes.

o **Talk openly about the needs of your kids:** Do you have a special needs child that needs particular schooling options? Do you have kids who are entering their last two years of the IB diploma program and hence cannot be moved before they are through? Did your kids have a hard time handling your previous move? Sometimes, delaying a move for the kids' education and stability – and timing it accordingly – is crucial.

o **Consider the effect a new language may have on your multilingual family:** As a MOLA Family, are you likely to turn down an expat posting because of a language issue? If your home language setup means you already speak many languages at home, or if your children cannot continue their education in their academic language – point out these concerns. If your home languages are French and Vietnamese, and you rely on your kids to learn English at school, then moving to a Spanish-speaking school in Colombia will pose an extra challenge for you and your family. If your company cannot offer you international schooling and you are forced to put your child in a local school, how will your child cope with the change in the academic language? Discuss this challenge with the company sending you abroad and how you may work around it.

o **Discuss the challenges brought forth by repeated expatriation:** You may be moving to Sao Paulo, but you still need your bank account in Dubai to remain open. Wealth management is an aspect that many companies underestimate. As a MOLA Family, it is possible and likely that you have income/wealth from different countries and need to be able to manage this effectively, while being aware and informed of how a potential move may impact your finances. Can you still contribute to a higher education fund you have set up for your children in the US, even if you are not a

US resident? There are many questions to discuss because serial expatriation poses incredible complexities in terms of wealth management for MOLA Families.

○ **Explore your options for retirement planning:** For MOLA Families who move around a lot, retirement planning is not easy to manage. How do you plan for retirement if you do not have a clear home base or a social security network in one country to rely on? This is an important conversation to have with your company. Are you eligible for a company-sponsored retirement plan?

○ **Discuss a repatriation scenario:** As discussed, MOLA Families may not have one clear-cut country to be repatriated to. After your current expatriation is over, where do you repatriate to? Your country? Your partner's country? The location of your company headquarters? Ensure repatriation options are discussed actively and that they make sense – not just on paper, but for your MOLA family. It is important to discuss the 'repatriation question' because in today's uncertain labor market, repatriation is always an option to fall back on.

○ **Ask for spousal career support:** Moving your family across continents often means that your spouse may have to give up work. This causes gender inequality and often forces mobile families into traditional gendered roles. Show your mola by actively asking for spousal support. Careers form a big part of our identity and the opportunity for active employment could make the difference between a successful posting abroad and an unhappy or stressful posting. If you are an expat spouse, ask if you can receive any help towards setting up your own business or entrepreneurial idea. Ask about help to secure an employment visa. Ask if you can receive career development assistance in setting up your own portable business. Amel Derragui, founder of Tandem Nomads, specializes in advising expat spouses how to build their portable businesses and explains: "Companies should be more involved in facilitating the integration of expat partners and considering their needs within the expatriation package. Their rights and status should be as much of a priority as the logistical aspects of relocation."

- **Ask for language support:** Many companies offer language classes or learning courses as a support when they move you to a country where you do not speak the local language. If you do not receive the support, then actively ask for language courses, because learning the language can help stitch your mola together. Learning the local language can help you feel more settled and at home in your new location.

- **Request annual home leave:** Many international companies and organizations offer their employee (and the family) an annual leave to their home country. Of course, as a MOLA Family, this may not necessarily be so clear-cut if you and your family have more than one home country. Mention this and discuss various options as to how and where you would like to take your 'home' leave. Don't be afraid of showing your mola as you discuss the prospect of a home leave.

SHOWING YOUR MOLA TO RELOCATION AGENCIES

Relocation agencies and global mobility specialists are often hired to help MOLA Families in their relocation process. It is vital as a MOLA Family to actively show your mola, by discussing who you are, what your requirements are, what will help you to settle in your new country and what kind of help/assistance you would find particularly useful.

- **Ask for on-the-ground relocation assistance:** One of the first things I request for my MOLA Family during a move is on-the-ground relocation assistance in processing paperwork such as obtaining residence permits, employment visas, driver license conversion to the local equivalent and more. This is so because given our complex backgrounds and nationalities, it can be a challenge trying to explain to a government office in Dubai, that while you look Pakistani, you are in the country on your Italian passport with your residence visa which is sponsored under your German husband's employment visa, but your American driver's license has expired so how do you obtain a local UAE license? A relocation agency can help schedule appointments with you (especially if you do not speak the local language or require help to do so) and can help speed up the process by sending documentation in advance, and so on.

- **Ask for support to find your new home:** Having help when it comes to finding a new house/apartment/condo in your new country can be immensely helpful. I have done international moves without having relocation assistance in terms of helping to find a place to live and it can be tough to figure it out by yourself, when you don't have an idea of the different types of home or neighborhoods or what the local real estate standards and norms are. This is the time to show your mola: ask for help, explain what kind of a home is important for you, what your family needs are and how best you can find a home that can help provide comfort during your time in a new country. In addition, ask for reliable contacts for carpenters, plumbers, electricians, gardeners or landscape companies that can help you get settled in quickly.

- **Ask for intercultural training:** Show your mola, by asking proactively for any intercultural training you may attend or receive to help you settle in. This could be a trip to the supermarket or the local market to give you an introduction to grocery shopping in your new country, or it could be an invitation to an informational session on local culture, norms and etiquette. Remember, the different cultures you are exposed to are woven into your mola fabric and thus, understanding the local culture is important and can help you adjust to your new surroundings in a healthy way.

SHOWING YOUR MOLA TO YOUR EXTENDED FAMILY

It can be easier to 'show' your mola to people you do not know, but it is often harder to show your mola to your extended family and friends during visits back home or in general conversations as you maintain your family ties and friendships. This is so because often those who know you the best or the longest will question you and your habits more. They may comment on how much you have changed after living abroad and you may find that you view your own country or your family and friends differently based on your time spent abroad. You may receive comments such as:

"Oh, your poor kids! If you keep moving to different countries, they will never know where they come from!"

"Isn't speaking so many languages at home confusing for you guys?"

"How come you are always traveling all over Europe, but you don't have time to come for a visit back home to the States?"

"Don't you feel like settling down somewhere?"

"When will you move back home?"

Often times, such questions or comments from your extended family or friends are a well-meaning attempt to relate to a life that is quite frankly unrelatable for them. When faced with questions or criticisms it may be your natural instinct to brush your 'otherness' under the rug. To try and show that your five years living in Paris has not changed you *that* much.

But I recommend that you do the complete opposite.

Show your mola to your extended family and friends. When you have combined different cultures, languages, traditions, nationalities and experiences of living around the world, you have something beautiful to show for it. Showing it can help others understand the journey you are on. They may still not be able to relate to it (and that's okay) but showing your mola is always a better option than hiding who you are. It may be difficult to have some conversations regarding parenting in different cultures and what is accepted versus not accepted or sharing your political opinions or discussing climate change or gun control, but acknowledging how you do things or why you think a certain way can be a good starting point.

What are some healthy ways in which you can show your mola to your extended family members and your friends? Here are some do's and don'ts:

Do's:

- Be honest about your MOLA Family and how your fusion, while wonderful, can also be messy. Explain how you tackle the mess.
- Explain how living in a certain culture (or cultures) has shaped the way you parent. Discuss the good aspects you have adopted or the challenging aspects of the local culture or your partner's culture that you struggle with. Talk about how you juggle different

expectations and in the end focus on doing what feels like a right way for your family.

- Offer to translate (if necessary) if it helps them to communicate with your multilingual family.

- Invite them to celebrate a new holiday or tradition you have adopted or love to celebrate in your host country.

- Invite them to visit you in your current country if possible.

- Cook new food that you eat as a result of your globally mobile lifestyle and ask them to join you or offer to teach them if they're interested in what you have learned.

- Give them a present or a souvenir that represents the country that you live in.

- Ask them to support you in any way they can. Perhaps they can help your children maintain their ties to your home country or culture.

- Be genuine and open about the challenges you face and the opportunities you enjoy through your multicultural, multilingual and multi-mobile lifestyle.

Don'ts:

- Don't champion one culture over another. Don't deride one culture in the face of another.

- Don't be ashamed of your bilingual kids, or of your multilingual family.

- Don't try to get your extended family or friends to agree with you on any topic; you don't need to 'convince' them about anything.

- Don't apologize for the fact that you have changed.

- Don't expect relationships to remain the same. Even if you had not left home and raised your family overseas, it is possible that your friendship may have changed anyway.

- Don't play the 'what if?' game: wondering about what things would have been like if you had not moved away.

- Don't expect your family life to be uncomplicated. Planning holidays and special events will require more negotiation and honest communication.

- Don't feel guilty about your choices.

SHOWING YOUR MOLA TO OTHER MOLA FAMILIES

MOLA Families are quick to recognize each other. When I found out that our new neighbors in Accra, Ghana, were a multicultural expat couple – the wife from Denmark, the husband from Ireland – who had just moved over from Kazakhstan with their three Danish-Irish-American children, I was excited. A MOLA Family as neighbors is a precious gift! Although we are not from the same countries or have even lived in the same places, we recognize that just like us they are a MOLA Family too.

Showing your mola to other MOLA Families feels natural and good. Discussing how you are building a life around different cultures, languages, nationalities and experiences of living around the world can feel less overwhelming when you can talk to someone else who 'gets it.' It can also help you forge a bond over your common MOLA identity.

Here are some ways in which you can 'show' your mola to other MOLA Families:

- Talk about your experience of mixing different cultures in your family. What part have you found the hardest? What part is the best?

- Share your journey of raising bilingual/multilingual kids but be respectful if the other MOLA Family has struggled with encouraging bilingualism or multilingualism in their family. Listen to their challenges and provide support instead of judgment.

- Not all MOLA Families are the same or face the same issues. Practice empathy and kindness when hearing another MOLA Family's story.

- Try to discover your new host country together and help each other appreciate and process the good, bad and ugly aspects of your new adventure.

- Learn from each other's experiences.

- Share what you know about stitching a MOLA Family together. Share your MOLA toolbox (Mix, Order, Layer and Adventure) and see what parts the other MOLA Family can relate to.

Often times MOLA Families also encounter particularly challenging circumstances such as a separation, divorce or death in the family. These major experiences can affect the dynamics of a MOLA Family and how it functions. Be respectful of other MOLA Families. Mixing cultures, speaking in different languages and combining several different identities into one family is never a smooth process.

SHOWING YOUR MOLA UPON RE-ENTRY/REPATRIATION

Often times, it is hardest to show your mola when you repatriate to one of your 'home' countries. This is so because of the need to 'fit in' or an attempt not to highlight your international life, your diversity, or your different identity than those in your hometown.

"Some of us, upon returning home, turn our tapestry over, hide the brilliance of its colors and its uniqueness, deny our heritage or reveal it to few. Perhaps this is done to blend in and gain acceptance, perhaps to deny the impact of loss – perhaps because frankly, it just seems easier," explained Norma McCaig, while addressing Third Culture Kids in her foreword to the first edition of the book *The Third Culture Kid Experience: Growing Up Among Worlds* by Ruth E. Van Reken and David C. Pollock.

Repatriation or re-entry is a key time when MOLA Families face a lot of questions and soul searching about their new identities. If their previous identity revolved around their globally mobile lifestyle, then how does that impact their new lives as repats who return to one of their home countries 'for good'?

"Re-entry shock feels like you are wearing contact lenses in the wrong eyes. Everything looks almost right," notes author Robin Pascoe in her book *Homeward Bound: A Spouse's Guide to Repatriation*. Many are tempted to brush their international experiences under the rug. This is partly due to the fact that the people around you are not able to relate to you and your foreign experiences. Partly because while your friends and family may have been prepared to hear your stories of "that time I took the wrong metro in Copenhagen" during your visits back home, they expect that now you live here, these stories should get fewer and fewer as you adjust to life back home. Many may perceive your stories of living abroad as attempts at bragging, expecting you to just erase the years of your life, which of course is impossible.

Showing your mola after repatriation or at the time of re-entry can be particularly painful. It can be difficult to talk about a life that is now in the past. But it is necessary. Perhaps even more so because you may now face the 'hidden immigrant' reality. Because now that you look and sound like everyone else, people expect you to fit in, to pick up from where you left and to have an easy time adjusting to your home country.

Often the focus is on 'fitting in' at the time of re-entry, and learning how to fit back into a society and culture that you once lived in. As a MOLA Family, it is important that you understand your mola, and are not afraid of showing it. Therefore, instead of using repatriation as a time to fit in, it can be the perfect opportunity to 'show' your mola as a way to connect your multi-layered identities.

Here are some ways for MOLA Families to 'show' their mola upon repatriation or re-entry into their home country:

- Embrace all the ways in which you and your family have changed since you left home and during your time abroad.
- Acknowledge how your family culture has changed as a result of your moves.
- Display what habits you have acquired along your journey, which will 'stay' with you regardless of where you live.
- Decided which hobbies you will continue doing even though you are living back home again.
- Display photos or souvenirs from your life abroad in your home.
- Find a conversation class to continue a language you have learned during your time abroad (French, Spanish or Mandarin etc.).
- Continue a skill you have learned during your time abroad. Perhaps you lived abroad in Japan and learned how to do Ikebana (flower arrangements) which you can continue teaching or sharing even in your home country. Perhaps during your time in Italy, you learned how to make regional specialties which you can share with those interested in learning Italian cooking.
- Encourage your children to keep in touch with their friends, schools and teachers in various countries through Skype, WhatsApp, Facebook, and so on.

- Understand that while you and your spouse may be back in your passport country (or one of your passport countries), perhaps it is the first time your children have lived in their passport country. If so, it may not feel like home to them at all. How can you help them through this transition of learning about their home country?

- Cook certain foods and dishes that remind you of your time abroad. Food is a great way to keep your mola alive and feel connected to your previous experiences.

- Plan holidays or visits with your friends who you met while living in different countries. Reunions can help you connect with your friends and maintain those international connections.

- Don't pretend your years living abroad don't exist just to make others feel less boring. Teach your kids and yourself to share what you have learned. Prepare your extended family like grandparents, aunts, uncles, nieces, nephews, cousins, schools and teachers that your kids will be talking about the four years they lived in China - not to brag about living in China, but because that has simply been their life until now. Sharing about their life is far more beneficial to their growth and development, as opposed to never talking about their life overseas simply not to be perceived as bragging or in a misguided attempt to fit in.

- Teach your kids how to share their stories by tailoring their story to their audience. This is a unique skill that can help both children and adults adjust, particularly at re-entry time. Think about your audience before you answer. If someone who has not traveled much asks about your experience of living overseas, you are likely to be more general, less specific, so as not to alienate your listener. If another mobile family asks about your experience you are likely to go into more detail and more specifics comparing the pros and cons between living in Singapore and Dubai.

Perhaps the most important thing to remember is this: your repatriation journey will also become part of your mola eventually. As you know, your mola is never complete; it is constantly changing. Soon, you will add experiences of moving back home into a new layer that will be 'stitched' onto your mola, just like all the previous layers.

Repatriation is not a new journey, but just a continuation of the journey you were already on. Think of it as a new layer of fabric in your mola, and you will be excited to show it, to learn from it and to grow from it.

The most important thing to remember is this: your repatriation journey will also become part of your mola eventually. Soon, you will add experiences of moving back home into a new layer that will be 'stitched' onto your mola.

THE FIVE RULES FOR OWNING YOUR MOLA-NESS

1. WHEN IN DOUBT, REVEAL YOUR MOLA

Revealing your mola can help you skip straight to the authentic part of who you are and what you stand for: diversity, tolerance and multiculturalism. When in doubt, reveal your mola. If a conversation on racial tension in North Carolina bothers you, reveal your mola: "Well as someone who lived in Nigeria for four years, I observed things differently based on my experience there…"

2. UNDERSTAND HOW YOUR MOLA IMPACTS YOUR PERSONAL AND PROFESSIONAL LIFE:

A mola is not a garment that you stitch and then fold neatly and put in your wardrobe. It is something you wear every single day. It is how you show yourself to the rest of the world. Understand how your mola impacts your personal life and your professional life daily. You may value diversity not just at home but also in the workplace. You may realize that the more multicultural your team is at work, the more effective you will be at problem-solving. Practice openly the ideas you stand for and believe in.

3. NEVER APOLOGIZE FOR YOUR MOLA:

When you find yourself in difficult situations or trying circumstances, take comfort in your MOLA identity. Never apologize for who you are or who your family is. You don't need to feel guilty for the fact that you can't relate to only one country or society but to many countries and many different societies. The more places you live in, the more places you have a chance to love. The more bonds you build, the more you can appreciate the world from different viewpoints. Don't apologize for your global identity, share it and use it well.

4. USE YOUR MOLA TO CONNECT WITH THOSE SIMILAR TO YOU AND THOSE DIFFERENT FROM YOU:

Build bridges. Connect people and cultures. Use your mola to connect with those similar to you and those who are very different from you. Seek commonality even if it is something big like a shared hometown or something small like a common interest for surfing, as the way to build bridges. Use your different languages to listen to the news from differing viewpoints. Often times the same news coming out of the Middle East is covered very differently by the Western media in English than on Al Jazeera in Arabic. Understand bias when you see it. Seek to destroy that bias by sharing what you know about a country, region, culture or society. Iran may look like a scary place on your neighbor's television set, but perhaps your neighbor would be surprised to hear about your two-week travel through Shiraz and Esfahan and how the locals made you feel welcome and cared for. Use your mola to make valuable human connections that transcend race, religion, boundaries and identities.

5. LIVE YOUR AUTHENTIC MOLA LIFE:

"To thine own self be true" Shakespeare reminded us, and the message still rings true for MOLA Families today. Live your authentic MOLA life; embrace both the chaos and the charisma, the challenges and the opportunities that this global life brings forward. Inject as much color as you can into your mola, the more layers the better. Live this life with humility, grace and gratitude.

CHAPTER SUMMARY

1. By 'showing' your mola and your MOLA Family, you are acknowledging and embracing your life story.

2. It is important to 'show' your mola to schools when you are deciding on the right educational environment and support for your children. Showing your mola can help you choose a school that is the right 'fit.'

3. Show your mola to international companies responsible for sending you abroad and to relocation agencies assigned to help you abroad. Both can contribute to making a smoother transition and lower the risk of failure or an assignment being cut short.

4. Show your mola to your extended family and help them understand how you have blended different cultures and traditions in your family. Show your mola to other MOLA Families and use it as a chance to bond, reflect and grow from each other's experiences.

5. To own your MOLA-ness, it is important to reveal your mola when in doubt, understand how your mola impacts your personal and professional life, never apologize for your mola, use your mola to connect with people similar to you and different from you and live your authentic MOLA life no matter where you go.

ACTIVITY: HOW DO YOU ADVOCATE FOR YOUR MOLA FAMILY?

Advocating for your mola means showing your MOLA Family to those around you but taking it a step further; it means standing up for the ideals and beliefs that you believe in and practice as a family.

What issues do you care about, based on your multicultural, multilingual and multi-mobile family?

- The issues I care about as a **multicultural** family:

- The issues I care about as a **multilingual** family:

- The issues I care about as a **multi-mobile** family:

What actions have you taken to advocate for your MOLA Family?

What actions can you take in the future to advocate for MOLA Families?

For help or inspiration, here are some of my answers:

The issues I care about are:

- **As a multicultural family:**

  - Cross-cultural families through marriage.
  - The commonalities between growing up as a TCK and a CCK.
  - What to do when you fall in love with someone from a different religion.
  - The rights of Muslim women to marry non-Muslim men.

- **As a multilingual family:**

  - The clear hierarchy of world languages; why does this exist? Why is a language like German more widely admired and encouraged than a language like Urdu?
  - Should parents worry about what language is more 'useful' to pass on to their kids or which language helps to maintain ties to their culture and identity?

- **As a multi-mobile family:**

  - What are the differences between expats and migrants and immigrants?
  - Why are refugee and immigrant families never part of the discussion on moving or addressed in forums on global mobility?
  - The debate on immigration and the rights of asylum seekers.

For my part, I have tried to raise awareness on several of these issues through my writing. I have written about migrant workers, presented their stories on a conference for globally mobile families and collaborated with organizations and startups in Dubai to support initiatives that talk about moving, beyond the expat experience. I will continue to write in support of multiculturalism, diversity and tolerance in our societies and continue to write about the needs of all people who move – under varying circumstances and propelled by different forces.

CONVERSATION STARTERS

Here are a few conversation starters for you and your family to answer, perhaps over a weekend family dinner:

1. **As a MOLA Family, you may feel comfortable showing your mola to some people, and in particular situations.**

   - What are the typical situations in which you feel comfortable to reveal your MOLA-ness? For example, when meeting someone who has also lived outside of their home country?

2. **Revealing your mola may feel uncomfortable at times. Fear that the other party may not relate or will judge you can often be present.**

   - When does revealing your mola feel tricky?
   - In what situations do you wish you could just 'fit in'?

3. **Advocating for your mola can feel daunting.**

   - What kind of support do you wish you had from family and friends?
   - What resources or initiatives would you join/support or like to volunteer your time for?

GLOSSARY
OF TERMS

· ·

There are a lot of technical terms and acronyms used when talking about globally mobile families and cross-cultural experiences. Understanding what they mean, and how they differ contributes to the understanding of this book.

Adult Third Culture Kid (ATCK)
An adult who grew up as a TCK and spent a significant portion of their life (before the age of 18) outside their passport country. An ATCK may or may not continue to live a globally mobile life as an expatriate adult.

Bilingual
Being bilingual means being able to communicate in two languages. The best definition of being bilingual is by bilingualism specialist Francois Grosjean: "Some bilinguals are dominant in one language, others do not know how to read and write one of their languages, others have only a passive knowledge of a language and finally a small minority have equal and perfect fluency in their two languages. What is important to keep in mind is that bilinguals are very diverse, as are monolinguals."

Cross-Cultural Kid (CCK)
A person who meaningfully interacts with two or more cultures during

childhood. Children born to parents from two different countries can be cross-cultural kids, as can children born to immigrant parents in a new country different than the parents' home country.

Expatriate (expat)

A person temporarily residing in a country other than their native country. Like a migrant worker, an expat often chooses to live abroad for better working conditions or a career opportunity. Expats often have time-bound employment contracts with implications for tax, savings, retirement, education and pension.

Hidden Immigrant

Someone who looks and sounds the same as everyone else in their home country, but due to a TCK upbringing or a life lived overseas, is not quite as native as the natives.

Home Country

This is the country of which a person is a national and for which they hold a passport. Many people who live cross-culturally have never lived in their home country or may have only visited it on family trips with their parents.

Host Country

This is the country and culture an expatriate lives in as a foreigner.

Immigrant

A person who moves to a foreign country with the intention of settling there permanently.

MOLA Family

A family that stitches together its own metaphorical mola using its multicultural influences as the fabric of its shirt, its multilingual make-up as the thread to sew the shirt together and its multi-mobile experiences to produce the different layers and ultimately provide the design of its mola. A MOLA Family is also one that uses the MOLA toolbox (Mix, Order, Layer, Adventure) to thrive in their globally mobile life.

Monolingual
A person who speaks or communicates in only one language.

Monocultural
A person who is influenced by a single culture – they are born in their parents' native countries and live their whole life there.

Migrant Worker
A person who moves from one place to another to find work or better living conditions. Often migrant workers leave their families in their home countries while they work in a different country and send money back home.

Multilingual
A person who can communicate in more than one language, either actively (through speaking, writing or signing), or passively (through listening, reading or perceiving).

Multicultural
A person can be multicultural in many ways. If they have more than one cultural influence within their family, they are multicultural. If they live outside of their native country (as an expat or an immigrant, for example) and are constantly interacting with more than one culture (such as the culture of their host country) they are also multicultural. Of course, it is also possible to be multicultural by having more than one culture at home and outside the home.

Re-entry/Repatriation

Repatriation or re-entry is the process of returning to one's passport country. For cross-cultural families who may have more than one passport country, repatriation is a tricky issue, since repatriation for one member of the family may not be a repatriation for their spouse, or other members of the family.

Third Culture Adult (TCA)

A person who lives as an expatriate for a long time, with the first international move occurring after age 18. This may also include adults who only spent a short time abroad as children (and do not identify as TCKs), and later spent a long period as an expatriate in adulthood.

Third Culture Kid (TCK)

A child who has spent a significant portion of their life before the age of 18 outside their passport country. Generally speaking a child who spends three or more years abroad will identify as a TCK.

THE MOBILE FAMILY SURVEY 2018

· ·

I ran *'The Mobile Family Survey'* from March until May 2018. The purpose was to reach out to multicultural, multilingual and multi-mobile families living all over the world, to get a sense of their family life and the particular challenges and opportunities they faced. Criteria for participants were:

- At least one international move as a family, and/or
- More than one language spoken at home, and/or
- More than one culture present at home.

EXECUTIVE SUMMARY OF THE SURVEY

Participants were asked to state their age group, their name (or if they preferred a pseudonym), their nationalities, their partner's nationalities, the countries in which they had lived (both by themselves and as a family), the languages they and their partner spoke, the number of children they had, and when and where their children were born to get a sense of their overall family history. Participants extended their explicit consent for their data and case studies to be used only for the purpose of this book either under their name or a pseudonym. Hence all case studies presented in this book are real and factual, although some names may have been changed upon the survey participant's request.

I surveyed a total of 110 families and went into depth to understand what parts of their mobile lives presented the biggest challenges and the biggest opportunities. I encouraged participants to share anecdotal examples of issues they encountered and mention other issues if not already included in the survey. A selection of these anecdotes were used as case studies in each chapter to form the questions and answers that the experts responded to.

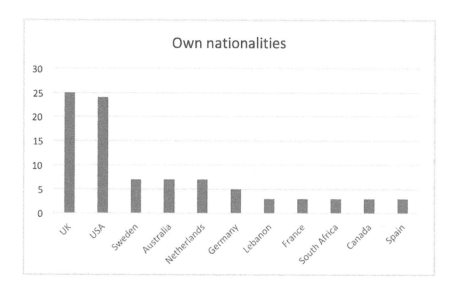

Additional nationalities (count of 2 or less):
Argentina, Austria, Bahrain, Belgium, Bulgaria, Colombia, Denmark, Finland, Greece, Guatemala, Hungary, India, Ireland, Israel, Italy, Latvia, Lithuania, Namibia, New Zealand, Pakistan, Panama, Poland, Portugal, Romania, Russia, Senegal, Switzerland, Thailand, Venezuela, Vietnam.

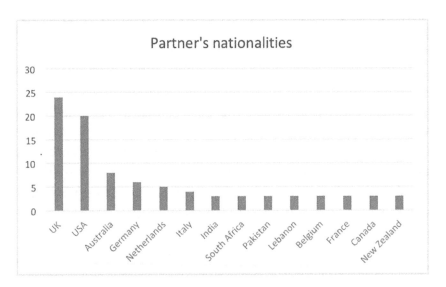

Additional nationalities (count of 2 or less):

Argentina, Bahrain, Brazil, China, Denmark, Egypt, Faroe Islands, Honduras, Iran, Iraq, Ireland, Israel, Madagascar, Malaysia, Mauritius, Mexico, Namibia, Palestinian Territories, Philippines, Portugal, Serbia, Spain, Sweden, Switzerland, Thailand, Uruguay, Venezuela.

KEY FINDINGS

The Mobile Family Survey showed:

Percentage of participants with more than one nationality: 19%

Percentage of participants with more than two nationalities: 3%

Percentage of participants married to someone from a different nationality: 58%

LANGUAGES

Participants were asked to list their first, second, third and fourth native languages. They were also asked to list which languages they had acquired later in life. They were then asked to share their partner's native languages and which languages their partners acquired later in life.

a) Native languages of participants:

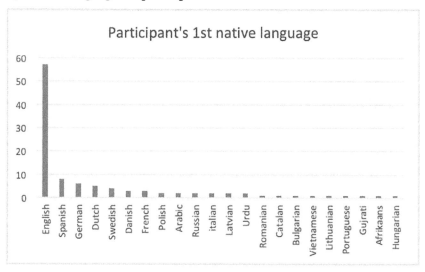

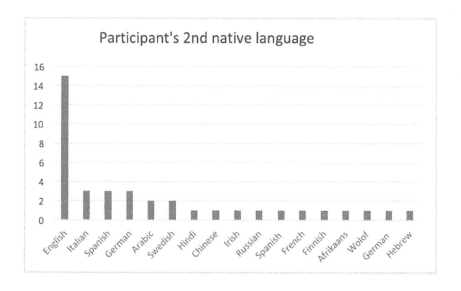

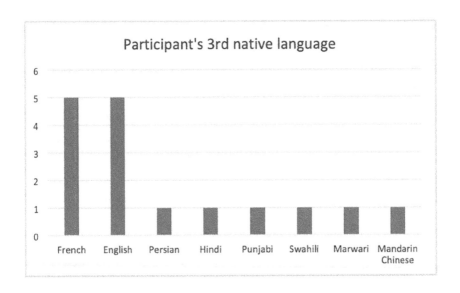

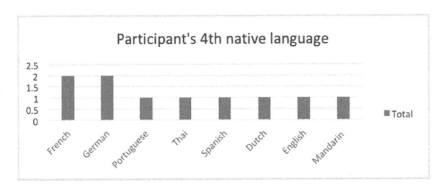

b) Acquired languages of participants (learned later in life):

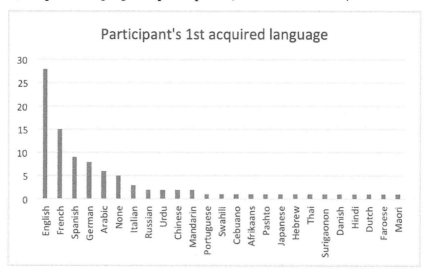

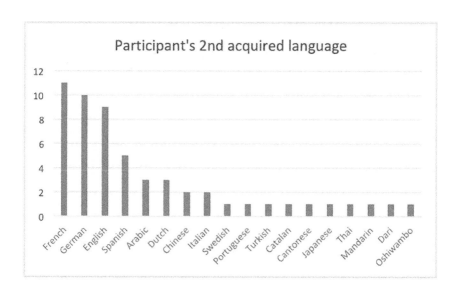

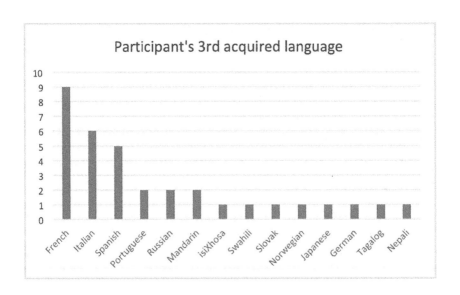

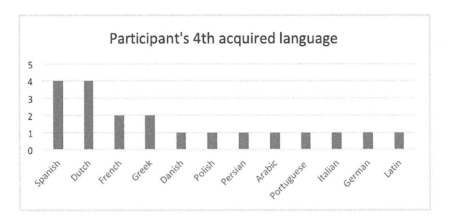

c) Partner's native languages:

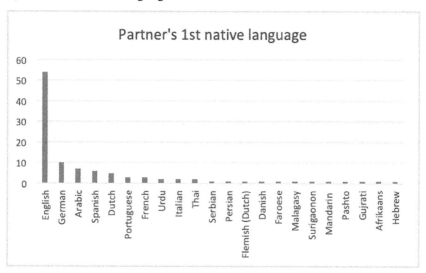

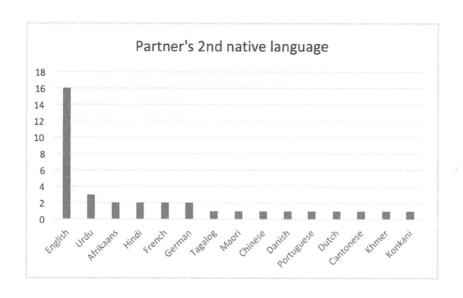

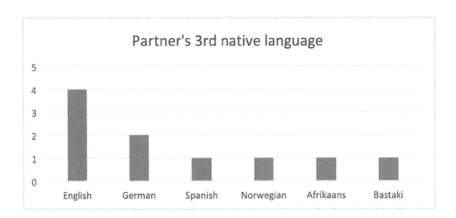

d) Partner's acquired languages

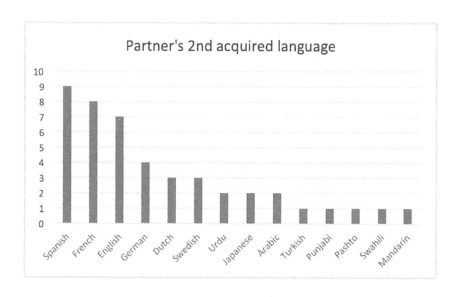

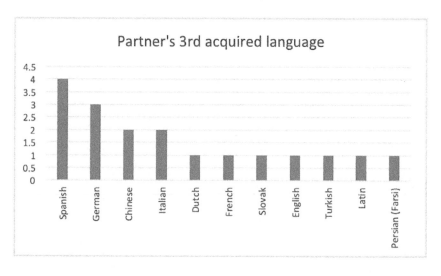

KEY FINDINGS

The Mobile Family Survey showed:

Percentage of participants who are monolingual: 67%

Percentage of participants who are bilingual: 17%

Percentage of participants who are multilingual: 16%

Percentage of monolingual families: 47%

Percentage of bilingual families: 32%

Percentage of multilingual families: 21%

MOBILITY

Participants were asked to share which countries and cities they had lived in both individually and as a couple (the list of countries was rather long, please see the Appendix).

The Mobile Family Survey showed:

Percentage of participants who had made one international move: 19%

Percentage of participants who made two international moves: 17%

Percentage of participants who made three or more international moves: 38%

Percentage of families who had made one international move: 22%

Percentage of families who had made two international moves: 24%

Percentage of families who had made three or more international moves: 43%

CHALLENGES OF GLOBALLY MOBILE FAMILIES

Participants were presented with 10 challenges and asked to rank these as they applied to their family on a scale of 1 to 10, with the most difficult challenge scoring a 10 and the least difficult challenge scoring a 1. Participants were also asked to list any additional challenges they may face. They were then asked to explain the challenge they picked as the most difficult and how/why it impacted their family.

These were the challenges presented in the survey:

Race: Your family members do not look like one another and your children may feel conflicted as to which race they belong to.

Religion: You and your partner have different religions and struggle to decide how to raise your children.

Language: You are raising your children bilingually or multilingually in and outside the home.

Culture: You struggle to reconcile two or more cultures and different cultural expectations in bringing up your family.

Identity: You try to reconcile multiple identities in your family.

Belonging: Your family members experience a split sense of belonging to more than one culture or country.

Sense of home: Home is a different place for some of your family members.

Family traditions: You struggle to decide which family traditions to adopt and celebrate in your family, while living in a foreign culture.

Unresolved grief: You struggle to help your children deal with their unresolved grief at moving countries and to help them face their tangible and intangible losses during an international relocation.

Dealing with in-laws and extended families: You face cultural expectations from in-laws or relatives which may not apply for your cross-cultural family. Traditions around birth, marriage or death may vary.

The Mobile Family Survey showed that participants found race and religion to be the hardest challenges faced when blending their multicultural families.

This was followed by unresolved grief in helping their children transition through an international relocation.

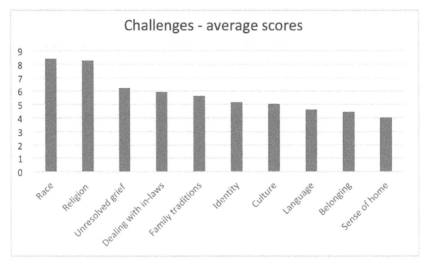

OPPORTUNITIES OF GLOBALLY MOBILE FAMILIES

Participants were presented with 10 opportunities and asked to rank these as they applied to their family on a scale of 1 to 10, with the most difficult opportunity scoring a 10 and the least difficult opportunity scoring a 1. Participants were also asked to list any additional opportunities they may face. They were then asked to explain the opportunity they picked as the most important they enjoyed and how/ why it contributes to their family happiness.

These were the opportunities presented in the survey:

Diversity: Your family can experience diversity either inside the home, or outside the home, or both.

A global outlook: Your family grows up with a global outlook. Your family members don't live their lives within walls and borders.

Access to many cultures: Your family can simultaneously access many cultures and understand global perspectives from varying viewpoints.

Communication advantages: Being bilingual/multilingual gives your family a communication edge and they can use their multiple languages for various purposes such as increased competitiveness in the labor market.

Empathy: You and your children grow up learning to practice empathy for others, given your constant exposure to new and different people.

Resilience and adaptability: You and your children learn to be resilient in the face of moving and new international experiences. You and your children adapt well to change and new surroundings.

Travel: You and your children have increased opportunities to travel the world.

Breaking barriers and boundaries: Your family learns how to break barriers and overstep boundaries. You try to find something in common with everybody and do not let differences in race, class or backgrounds hold you back.

Job opportunities: Your family enjoys access to increased job opportunities because of their multiple nationalities, languages, intercultural expertise and global experiences.

Linguistic empathy: Your family practices linguistic empathy inside the home and outside - tolerance, understanding and respect of the different languages you encounter at home and outside.

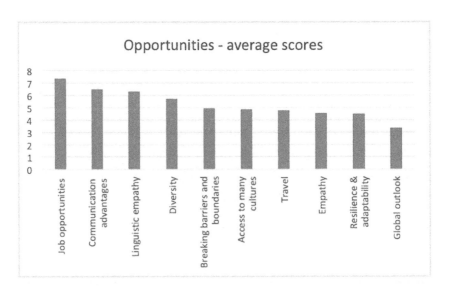

The Mobile Family Survey showed that participants enjoyed increased job opportunities because of their multiple nationalities, languages, intercultural expertise and global experiences, followed by communication advantages, linguistic empathy and diversity.

CONCLUSION

The Mobile Family Survey showed that multicultural, multilingual and multi-mobile families face many challenges in living their globally mobile lives, but they also enjoy several opportunities.

APPENDIX

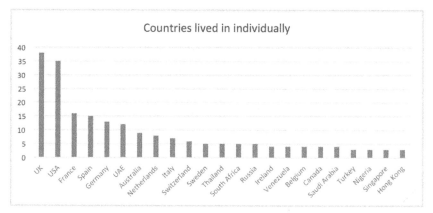

Additional countries (count of 2 or less):
Argentina, Austria, Bangladesh, Belarus, Bosnia, Brazil, Brunei, Bulgaria, Chile, China, Colombia, Costa Rica, Cuba, Denmark, Dominican Republic, DRC, Egypt , Finland, Gibraltar, Greece, Guatemala, Honduras, Hungary, India, Indonesia, Iraq, Israel, Jamaica, Japan, Jordan, Kenya, Latvia, Lebanon, Libya, Lithuania , Luxembourg, Madagascar, Malawi, Malaysia, Mali, Namibia, New Zealand, Pakistan, Panama, Paraguay, Peru, Philippines, Poland, Romania, Senegal, Syria, Taiwan, Tanzania, Turkmenistan, Vietnam, Yemen, Zimbabwe.

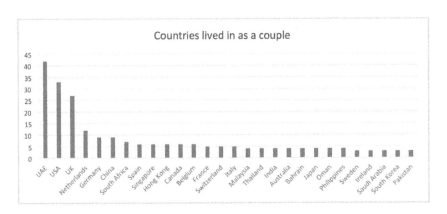

Countries lived in as a couple

Additional countries (count of 2 or less):

Afghanistan, Albania, Austria, Brazil, Brunei, Burkina Faso, Cambodia, Colombia, Costa Rica, Denmark, Dominican Republic, DRC, Egypt, Ethiopia, Ghana, Honduras, Hungary, Israel, Jamaica, Jordan, Kenya, Kosovo, Madagascar, Mali, Mexico, Morocco, Nepal, New Zealand, Norway, Palestinian Territories, Peru, Portugal, Romania, Slovakia, St. Lucia, Tanzania, Turkey, Vietnam.

MEET THE EXPERTS

· ·

SUNDAE SCHNEIDER-BEAN

 Sundae is an intercultural strategist and a solution-oriented coach who specializes in minimizing time to adapt and maximizing satisfaction and success abroad. Sundae helps individuals and organizations expedite success, create meaningful connections abroad and at home, and cherish the experience. As an intercultural strategist, Sundae fast-tracks clients' adaptation and guides them through their most hefty cross-cultural challenges to make important changes that last. Sundae's work has been featured by the U.S. State Department in the Foreign Service Assignment Notebook, InterNations, and ExpatWoman, among others.

Rated #1 on iTunes in Places & Travel, Sundae's podcast Expat Happy Hour offers funny and heartfelt insights on work, travel, and life abroad. Episodes range from fitting in and living abroad without regrets to expat fatigue and can be found on iTunes and her website at www.sundaebean.com. From serving clients hailing from over 60 countries and six continents as well as from her own 18+ years abroad,

Sundae deeply understands the challenges of expatriate life. Sundae is an American and together with her Swiss husband and two kids, her family has lived in the US, Switzerland, Burkina Faso and South Africa. She currently resides in Pretoria, South Africa.

www.sundaebean.com

 @SundaeSchneiderBeanLLC

 @SundaeBean

 linkedin.com/in/sundaeschneiderbean

Expat Happy Hour podcast:
Search for Expat Happy Hour on iTunes

Expats on Purpose Group:
 /groups/expatsonpurpose

TRISHA CARTER

Trisha Carter is an Intercultural Specialist, helping people from different cultures work effectively together. As an Organisational Psychologist she coaches, trains and counsels leaders and their teams to work well and live well globally – to manage the challenges of communicating, managing people and adapting to living and working in new locations.

Since beginning work in this area Trisha has emphasized the importance of the family in an executive's global transition including partners in pre-departure training programs. She has also developed programs for partners and children. Trisha's face-to-face training business, Trans Cultural Careers, has been providing training and coaching to expatriates and their families, multicultural teams and global business executives for over 17 years. She has delivered training and presentations in Australia, New Zealand, Papua New Guinea, China, USA, The Netherlands and the UK.

Trisha has also founded an online support system with resources for expatriates and their families. The Cultural Intelligence Collective provides extensive cultural adaptation eBooks, webinars, and interviews via www.cicollective.com.

One of the key resources Trisha has developed, with her co-author Rachel Yates, is a guided journal for adapting to life overseas – *Finding Home Abroad*. Trisha and Rachel believe journaling is a life changing tool that can travel with you wherever you go.

Trisha has a master's degree in Psychology and is a Certified Cultural Intelligence Facilitator. She became interested in culture and the impacts of global transitions while living in China with her husband and young children in the 90s. While Sydney is currently home, her birthplace of New Zealand still has a special place in her heart. She has also served on the Families in Global Transition (FIGT) Board since October 2017.

www.cicollective.com

Finding Home Abroad:
www.expatjournals.com

Families in Global Transition:
www.figt.org

JERRY JONES

Jerry is the American cross-cultural trainer, speaker, writer and founder behind The Culture Blend; a website where he talks about blending cultures both personally and professionally and shares thoughts on expat life, repatriation and transition. He and his family have expatriated from the United States to China, repatriated to the United States and then expatriated once again to China. When he lived in Asia for the first time, he was the Executive Director and lead trainer for a company that helped people navigate the challenges of a shrinking world. He currently works as a Transition Specialist with Leadership Development International and conducts training and coaching for individuals and families who are transitioning to life as outsiders, whether it be becoming an expat in China or trying to remember how to function in their own country.

Jerry and his wife have adopted their two kids (one from China and one from the US) and together their multicultural and multi-ethnic family currently resides in Qingdao, China. Jerry is the author of the three books: *99 Questions for Global Families, 99 Questions for Global Friends* and *The Day Grandma Got Us Kicked Out of Mexico – and other fun stories about life as a bumbling American foreigner.*

www.thecultureblend.com

E-Books and paperback:
99 Questions for Global Families – www.thecultureblend.com
99 Questions for Global Friends – www.thecultureblend.com
The Day Grandma Got Us Kicked Out of Mexico; and other fun stories about life as a bumbling American foreigner – viewbook.at/TheDayGrandma

RITA ROSENBACK

Rita Rosenback is a Family Language Coach, speaker and author. Her book *Bringing up a Bilingual Child* is an easy-to-read guide navigating readers across the *"Seven C's of Multilingual Parenting: Communication, Confidence, Commitment, Consistency, Creativity, Culture and Celebration."*

Rita's website, Multilingual Parenting, has more than 300 posts and Q&As on the topic of raising children to speak more than one language. She regularly holds live Facebook sessions where she answers parents' questions. The sessions are free to attend on her Facebook page and she also has an active Facebook group for anyone interested.

Rita is the current vice-president of FIGT – Families in Global Transition, a board member of Multicultural Kid Blogs and also works as an Intercultural Youth Trainer.

Rita was born a Finn-Swede and after stays in Germany and India she now lives in the UK. She has two multilingual adult daughters and is currently helping to pass on Swedish to her grandson. In her free time Rita enjoys spending time with her grandson and hiking in the Peak District with her husband, always with a camera at the ready.

Rita offers individual family language coaching including tailor-made Family Language Plans and can be contacted via email.

www.multilingualparenting.com

rita.rosenback@multilingualparenting.com

📘 @multilingual.parenting

📘 /groups/multilingualparenting

Book:
Bringing Up a Bilingual Child – viewbook.at/BilingualChild

Families in Global Transition:
www.figt.org

Multicultural Kid Blogs:
www.multiculturalkidblogs.com

SOILE PIETIKÄINEN

Soile is a sociologist specializing in bilingual family interaction. She has developed a methodology for activating languages that children have never begun to speak or have stopped speaking. She is the founder and director of Bilingual Potential, an ethical business that provides services to support every child's right to learn and use the language(s) of their parents as defined in Article 30 of UNCRC. She believes that in bilingualism, learning more is easier than learning less and that using our multiple languages at home should be effortless and joyful.

Her upcoming book, Bilingual Cake Book, explains why some families are successful in bilingual parenting, what might be holding us back and how to make things better. Through the Bilingual Cake blog you can also find free content and buy services for bilingual and multilingual families.

Soile has a PhD in Education, focused on bilingualism at the University of London, whereby she studied the social factors behind minority language maintenance and erosion in bilingual families. Her solutions are often different from the mainstream bilingualism advice because they are based on a new area of research – the sociology of bilingual family interaction. She has appeared on several media outlets such as Sisu Radio – Sweden, The Guardian, BBC Radio 4, Helsingin Sanomat, YLE and MTV3 to share her views on bilingual childrearing. She is also the current co-chair of Families in Global Transition (FIGT) UK.

Soile is from Finland. She is Finnish-English-Italian trilingual and lives in London with her Italian husband and native trilingual teenagers.

www.bilingualpotential.org

🅕 @bilingualcake

🅸🅽 linkedin.com/in/soile-pietikäinen-93647bba

UTE LIMACHER-RIEBOLD

 Dr. Ute Limacher-Riebold was lecturer in Linguistics at the Department of Romance Studies in Zurich for eight years, and is a researcher in multilingualism, and Language Consultant and Intercultural Communication Trainer at Ute's International Lounge. She is native and nearly native in six languages and raises her three children with five languages. She advises parents about best practices on raising children with multiple languages by bridging between scientific research and families' interests and challenges.

With her personalized Family Language Plan© she helps families set and agree on short and long-term language goals, find the best solutions regarding language strategies, language resources, finding the right schools and maintaining the home languages, while fostering the community and school languages. When necessary, Ute mediates between parents, teachers and health practitioners, and trains teachers about best practices in multilingual classrooms.

www.utesinternationallounge.com

info@utesinternationallounge.com

 /groups/MultilingualFamilies

RUTH VAN REKEN

Ruth E. Van Reken is an American citizen, who grew up as a Third Culture Kid (TCK) in Nigeria, before raising her own family overseas in Liberia. She is a second generation Adult TCK and mother of three Adult TCKs. She writes and speaks internationally on issues related to global family living.

For over 30 years, Ruth has worked with families, educators and others in trying to help them understand issues TCKs face as globally mobile children. Her interest has expanded to see how lessons learned from those who have grown up cross-culturally with high mobility can apply to other groups of Cross-Cultural Kids (CCKs).

Ruth is the co-author of the famous book *Third Culture Kids: Growing Up Among Words together* with David C. Pollock and Michael V. Pollock and the author of the book *Letters Never Sent,* a journal through her own TCK childhood from hurt to healing. She is also the co-founder of Families in Global Transition, a welcoming forum for globally mobile individuals, families and those working with them.

www.crossculturalkid.org

Books:
Third Culture Kids: Growing Up Among Worlds – viewbook.at/TCKs
Letters Never Sent; A global nomad's journey from hurt to healing – viewbook.at/Letters

Families in Global Transition: www.figt.org

VALÉRIE BESANCENEY

Valérie is an Adult Third Culture Kid (ATCK). Originally Dutch, she grew up changing schools and countries four times by the time she graduated high school. As an adult, she has lived and worked in ten different countries before finally settling down in Switzerland.

Valérie holds a Master's in Education in Curriculum and Instruction from George Mason University and a Bachelor of Arts in English and German Literature. Valérie currently works as a primary school teacher at an international school in Switzerland.

Her books, B at Home: Emma Moves Again and My Moving Booklet are published by Summertime Publishing and are valuable resources for parents to use in preparing their young kids for an international move. Her writing addresses the impact of mobility on children and has been published on www.internationalschoolcommunity.com and she blogs on www.valeriebesanceney.com. She is also the current Program Chair for Families in Global Transition for 2019.

www.valeriebesanceney.com

Books:
B at Home: Emma Moves Again – viewbook.at/BatHome
My Moving Booklet – mybook.to/MyMovingBooklet

Families in Global Transition:
www.figt.org

KRISTIN LOUISE DUNCOMBE

Kristin Louise Duncombe is an American psychotherapist, life coach, and author who lives in Geneva, Switzerland. She has based her career on working with international and expatriate individuals and families following her own experience of growing up across Africa and Asia as the child of a US diplomat, and having lived internationally most of her adult life.

She is the author of the books Trailing: A Memoir and Five Flights Up, both memoirs that address, among other things, the specific challenges and idiosyncrasies of the expat existence. She has twenty solid years of experience working as a therapist and coach with individuals, couples, and families in the United States, East Africa, and Europe, and also provided the counseling services for the American University of Paris from 2008 until 2012. She works with people in her home office in Geneva, or by Skype or phone with people in different geographic areas all over the world. For more information or to get in touch with Kristin, please see her website.

www.kristinduncombe.com

Books:
Trailing: a Memoir - mybook.to/Trailing
Five Flights Up: Sex, Love and Family, from Paris to Lyon - viewbook.at/FiveFlightsUp

BIBLIOGRAPHY

Baker, Colin (2014). *A Parents' and Teachers' Guide to Bilingualism.* Multilingual Matters.

Baker, Colin (2011). *Foundations of Bilingual Education and Bilingualism,* 5th edition. Multilingual Matters.

Baker, Colin (2000). *The Care and Education of Young Bilinguals: An Introduction for Professionals.* Multilingual Matters.

Besanceney, Valérie (2014). *B at Home: Emma Moves Again.* United Kingdom: Summertime Publishing.

Crossman, Tanya (2016). *Misunderstood; The Impact of Growing Up Overseas in the 21st Century.* United Kindom: Summertime Publishing.

FIGT (2018) *A Reunion of Strangers: Words of Wisdom from the Families in Global Transitions Conference Community.* United Kingdom: Summertime Publishing.

Genesse, Fred (2015). *Myths About Early Childhood Bilingualism.* Canadian Psychology/Psychologie Canadienne, 56 (1), 6-15.

Genesee, Fred (2009). *Early Childhood Bilingualism: Perils and Possibilities.* Journal of Applied Research in Learning, 2 (Special Issue), 2, 1–21.

Grosjean, Francois (2010). *Bilingual: Life and Reality.* Harvard University Press.

Lemieux, Diane; Parker, Anne (2013). *The Mobile Life – A New Approach to Moving Anywhere.* Netherlands: XPat Media.

Ota, Douglas (2014). *Safe Passage: How Mobility Affects People & What International Schools Should Do about It.* United Kingdom: Summertime Publishing.

Meyer, Erin (2014). *The Culture Map: Decoding How People Think, Lead, and Get Things Done Across Cultures.* USA: Public Affairs.

Perrin, Michel (1999). *Magnificent Molas: The Art of the Guna Indians.* Paris: Flammarion.

Pascoe, Robin (2000). *Homeward Bound: A Spouse's Guide to Repatriation.* Canada: Expatriate Press Limited.

Pascoe, Robin (2006). *Raising Global Nomads.* Canada: Expatriate Press Limited.

Pollock, David C.; Van Reken, Ruth E.; Pollock, Michael V. (2017). *Third Culture Kids: Growing Up Among Worlds.* Third Edition. USA: Nicholas Brealey Publishing.

Pollock, David C.; Van Reken, Ruth E. (1999). *The Third Culture Kid Experience: Growing Up Among Worlds.* USA: Intercultural Press.

Rosenback, Rita (2014). *Bringing Up A Bilingual Child – How to Navigate the Seven C's of Multilingual Parenting: Communication, Confidence, Commitment, Consistency, Creativity, Culture and Celebration.* United Kingdom: Filament Publishing Ltd.

Tokuhama-Espinosa, Tracey (2001). *Raising Multilingual Children: Foreign Language Acquisition and Children.* USA: Bergin & Garvey.

Vlachos, Katia (2018). *A Great Move: How to survive and thrive in your expat assignment.* LID Publishing.

Online Articles and Studies Referenced

Anthony, Diedre (2015). 'Interview with an Expert in Multicultural Studies – Francis Wardle.' www.huffpost.com/entry/interview-with-an-expert_b_8452226

Berger, Kate (2017). 'Expat Kids: How to Spot If Your Child Is Not Settling In.' propertylistings.ft.com/propertynews/united-kingdom/5207-expat-kids-how-to-spot-if-your-child-is-not-settling-in.html

Cook, Vivian J. (2001). 'Requirements for a Multilingual Model of Language Production.' www.multilingualliving.com/2010/05/01/the-benefits-of-multilingualism/

Derragui, Amel (2015). 'Why Are Trailing Spouses' Challenges Such a Big Deal?' tandemnomads.com/blog/why-are-trailing-spouses-challenges-such-a-big-deal/

Grosjean, Francois (2010). 'Myths About Bilingualism.' www.francoisgrosjean.ch/myths_en.html

Jackson, Tyler (2008). 'What is a mola?' usmfreepress.org/2008/10/06/what-is-a-mola/

Language and Culture Website (2015). 'The Cultural Iceberg.'
www.languageandculture.com/cultural-iceberg

Limacher-Riebold, Ute (2018). 'Code Switching, What to Do, When Should I Worry?'
www.utesinternationallounge.com/code-switching-what-to-do-when-should-i-worry/

Lowry, Lauren. 'Bilingualism in Young Children: Separating Fact from Fiction.'
www.hanen.org/Helpful-Info/Articles/Bilingualism-in-Young-Children--Separating-Fact-fr.aspx

Mola: Art Form, Wikipedia.
en.wikipedia.org/wiki/Mola_(art_form)

Rosenback, Rita (2015). 'Two Parents, Two Languages – 2P2L, Double the Benefit of OPOL?'
multilingualparenting.com/2015/05/06/two-parents-two-languages-2p2l-double-the-benefits-of-opol/

Rosenback, Rita (2014). 'Bilingual Children: The Case for Consistency.'
multilingualparenting.com/2014/09/24/bilingual-children-consistency/

Shield Geo, 'Global Mobility: Reasons for International Assignment Failure and Managing Them.'
shieldgeo.com/global-mobility-reasons-for-international-assignment-failure-and-managing-them/

Sanblas Islands. 'How It's Made: Molas.'
sanblas-islands.com/news/how-its-made-molas/

Vlachos, Katia (2016). 'Dealing with Expat Divorce Part 1: Why It's Different for Expats.'
www.linkedin.com/pulse/dealing-expat-divorce-part-1-why-its-different-expats-katia-vlachos/

Wu, Alice (2015). 'Interview of Dr. Doug Ota and Book Review of Safe Passage.'
uydmedia.com/interview-of-dr-doug-ota-and-book-review-of-safe-passage-by-alice-wu/

YouTube Video: The Mola of Panama and Colombia.
www.youtube.com/watch?v=sA_ats3TwT0

RESOURCE LIST AND RECOMMENDED FURTHER READING:

· ·

(PUT TOGETHER WITH HELP FROM MY TEAM OF EXPERTS)

Books

Barron-Houwaert, Suzanne (2011). *Bilingual Siblings. Language Use in Families.* Multilingual Matters.

Braun, Andreas; Tony Cline (2014). *Language Strategies for Trilingual Families. Parents' Perspectives.* Multilingual Matters.

Brubaker, Cate; Cumberford, Doreen; Watts, Helen (2018). *Arriving Well: Stories about Identity, Belonging and Rediscovering Home After Living Abroad.* Kindle Edition.

Bushong, Lois (2013). *Belonging Everywhere & Nowhere: Insights into Counseling the Globally Mobile.* Mango Tree Intercultural Services.

Byalistok, Ellen (2003). *Language Processing in Bilingual Children.* CUP.

Duncombe, Kristin L. (2012). *Trailing: A Memoir.* CreateSpace.

Duncombe, Kristin L. (2016). *Five Flights Up: Sex, Love and Family, from Paris to Lyon*. CreateSpace.

Ferland, Lisa (2016). *Knocked Up Abroad: Stories of pregnancy, birth and raising a family in a foreign country*. Lisa Ferland.

Grosjean, Francois; Ping Li (2013). *The Psycholinguistics of Bilingualism*. Wiley Blackwell.

Gardner, Marilyn R. (2014). *Between Worlds: Essays on Culture and Belonging*. Doorlight Publications.

Harris, Jodi; Evans, Leah (2018). *Kids on the Move. 25 Activities to Help Kids Connect, Reflect and Thrive Around the World*. CreateSpace.

Iyer, Pico (2000). *The Global Soul: Jet Lag, Shopping Malls and the Search for Home*. Vintage Books.

Jaumont, Fabrice (2017). *The Bilingual Revolution. The Future of Education is in Two Languages*. TBR.

Janssen, Linda A. (2013). *The Emotionally Resilient Expat – Engage, Adapt and Thrive Across Cultures*. Summertime Publishing.

Melkonian, Lois (2015). *Hybrid: The Transformation of a Cross-Cultural People Pleaser*. Lois Melkonian.

Molinsky, Andy (2013). *Global Dexterity: How to Adapt Your Behavior Across Cultures without Losing Yourself in the Process*. Harvard Business Review Press.

O'Shaughnessy, Christopher (2014). *Arrivals, Departures and the Adventures In-Between*. Summertime Publishing.

Parfitt, Jo; Reichrath-Smith, Colleen (2013). *A Career in Your Suitcase*. 4th Edition, Summertime Publishing.

Parfitt, Jo; Wilson, Terry Anne (2018). *Monday Morning Emails: Six months, twelve countries, a thousand thoughts – two mothers share the journey of living a global life.* Summertime Publishing.

Pascoe, Robin (2009). *A Broad Abroad: The Expat Wife's Guide to Successful Living Abroad.* Expatriate Press Limited.

Pittman, Lisa; Smit, Diana (2011). *Expat Teens Talk: Peers, Parents and Professionals offer support, advice and solutions in response to Expat Life challenges as shared by Expat Teens.* Summertime Publishing.

Pollock, David C.; Van Reken, Ruth E.; Pollock, Michael V. (2017). *Third Culture Kids: Growing Up Among Worlds.* Third Edition. USA: Nicholas Brealey Publishing.

Romano, Dugan (2008). *Intercultural Marriage: Promises and Pitfalls.* Intercultural Press, a division of Nicholas Brealey Publishing.

Rockson, Tayo (2015). *The Ultimate Guide to TCK Living: Understanding the World Around You.*

Simens, Julia (2012). *Emotional Resilience and the Expat Child: Practical Storytelling Techniques That Will Strengthen the Global Family.* Summertime Publishing.

Van Reken, Ruth E. (2012). *Letters Never Sent: A Global Nomad's Journey from Hurt to Healing.* Summertime Publishing.

Vlachos, Katia (2018). *A Great Move: How to survive and thrive in your expat assignment.* LID Publishing.

Wiggins, Clara (2015). *The Expat Partner's Survival Guide.* Smashwords.

Wang, Xiao-lei (2008). *Growing Up with Three Languages: Birth to Eleven.* Multilingual Matters.

Zurer Pearson, Barbara (2008). *Raising a Bilingual Child. A step-by-step guide for parents.* Living Language.

Websites

For all aspects of multilingual life: www.multilingual-matters.com

For all aspects of bilingualism: www.bilingualism-matters.ppls.ed.ac.uk

The reality of living with two or more languages:
www.psychologytoday.com/intl/blog/life-bilingual

Francois Grosjean's website for learning another language,
biculturalism and applied linguistics: www.francoisgrosjean.ch

Founded by Dr. Barbara Schaetti, Cultural Detective is an intercultural
tool to enhance your intercultural expertise:
www.culturaldetective.com

Expat Child offers practical relocation advice to make overseas
relocation easy for the whole family: www.expatchild.com

Articles and information by expat women to help expat women
and their families meet new cultures: www.expatclic.com

A free website helping expatriate women from all nationalities
in any country in the world share experiences and advice:
www.expatwoman.com

The Expat Kids Club founded by Kate Berger provides a sense of
belonging to kids and is a safe-haven for those who might miss
stability in their life, due to international relocations:
www.expatkidsclub.com

Through sharing our local knowledge, Relocate Guru aims to support and encourage friendly and cohesive communities to help everyone feel like a local: www.relocateguru.io

This Netherlands-based website provides useful resources for those living and working in the Netherlands, Germany, France, Spain, and Belgium: www.expatica.com

For families and educators raising world citizens through arts, activities, crafts, food, language and love: www.multiculturalkidblogs.com

Chris O'Shaughnessy uses a unique blend of storytelling, humor and insight to engage people on cross-cultural understanding and globalization: www.chris-o.com

For missionary families living overseas: www.alifeoverseas.com

Ellen Mahoney began Sea Change Mentoring to help young adults identify and apply the skills acquired in their international backgrounds towards their career, academic and personal goals: www.seachangementoring.com

A resource-rich interactive website for adult TCKs and CCKs: www.tckidnow.com

A home for international creatives, founded by Mary Bassey – The Displaced Nation: www.thedisplacednation.com

Families in Global Transition hosts a yearly international conference on topics related to global family living: www.figt.org. It also has a researcher's network: www.figt.org/research_network

Founded by Jane Barron, Globally Grounded partners students, families and educators in effective cultural transition: www.globallygrounded.com

What Expats Can Do increases their involvement in their local communities to bring hope around the world: www.whatexpatscando.com

The Black Expat shares experiences, adventures and interviews related to being a black expat: www.theblackexpat.com

I Am a Triangle is a community for people living abroad to share their cross-cultural experiences and draw support from an international tribe: www.iamatriangle.com

Culturs Global Multicultural Magazine is an online magazine to promote cross-cultural excellence: www.culturs.guru

Beijing Kids is the essential international family resource in Beijing: www.beijing-kids.com

Global Nomads World offers consulting services for individuals before during and after transition, expat partner coaching, cross-cultural talks and repatriation support: www.globalnomadsworld.com

Blogs/Podcasts/Coaching

Communicating Across Boundaries: A blog by Marilyn Gardner that covers a wide variety of TCK issues and cross-cultural experiences. www.communicatingacrossboundariesblog.com

The Piri-Piri Lexicon: A blog by Annabelle Humanes as a linguist mum that covers multilingualism and raising CCKs around the world. www.thepiripirilexicon.com

Notes on a Boarding Pass: A travel blog by Terry Anne Wilson about exploring a love for travel while learning lessons from living all around the world. www.notesonaboardingpass.com

Knocked Up Abroad: A blog by Lisa Ferland sharing stories about multicultural parenting. www.knockedupabroad.com

The Bilingual Kidspot: A blog by Chontelle Bonfiglio about tips, strategies and resources for raising bilingual kids. www.bilingualkidspot.com

Expitterpattica: A blog by an adult TCK mom Lucille Abendanon raising three multicultural boys, sharing stories of living around the world. www.expitterpattica.com

Little Nomadas: A bilingual blog (Spanish/English) by a Venezuelan mom Flor Garcia offering tips, articles and resources on raising her multilingual and multicultural TCKs in Germany. www.littlenomadas.com

Monday Morning Emails: A blog by Jo Parfitt and Terry Anne Wilson, two global moms who write emails to each other every Monday about their expat lives, their empty nest and the questions around belonging, home and identity. www.mondaymorningemails.com

Expat Joy: A blog by Sandra Bissell about finding the joy in your expat life. www.expatjoy.com

World Tree Coaching: A blog by expat coach Jodi Harris on helping you live your best global life by staying mindful about your visions and goals. www.worldtreecoaching.com

Tandem Nomads: A podcast hosted by business and marketing expert Amel Derragui, aimed at helping expat partners thrive in their international assignments and advice on how to build a portable career. www.tandemnomads.com

Kid World Citizen: A blog by Becky Morales an ESL and Spanish teacher, raising five bilingual and multicultural kids and sharing ideas to teach kids about world cultures. www.kidworldcitizen.org

Two Fat Expats: a podcast hosted by Kirsty Rice and Nikki Moffitt about living a fat expat life and enjoying the adventures. www.twofatexpats.com

Mummy on My Mind: A blog by Zeyna Sanj, a British Indian expat who was born in Saudi Arabia and raising her multicultural family in Dubai. www.mummyonmymind.com

Copat Coaching: A coaching service by Dutch expat Margot based in Brunei, for expats around the world who want to grow personally and professionally. www.copatcoaching.com

Our Globetrotters: A blog about family travel, expat life, expat parenting and financial wellness of raising a family overseas. www.ourglobetrotters.com

Bicultural Mama: A blog by a Chinese-American mom raising a bicultural family in Long Island, New York. www.biculturalmama.com

Let the Journey Begin: A blog by Ilze Ievina, about a diary of a trilingual family living in Germany. www.letthejourneybegin.eu

Family Life in Spain: A blog by Lisa Sadleir about tips, experiences and resources on moving to Spain with children. www.familylifeinspain.com

Mama Tortuga: A blog by Johana Castillo-Rodriguez on raising a multicultural family after immigration to the United States. www.mamatortuga.org

Rafs World Travel: A blog by a British-Filipino family living in Saudi Arabia on a journey to show their son Raf the world. www.rafsworld.com

The Colours of Us: A blog by Svenja Gernand about sharing multicultural children's books and writing on diversity and bi-racial families. www.thecoloursofus.com

Olga Mecking: Multicultural writing on food, languages and living abroad by Olga Mecking a Polish journalist and translator living with her German husband in the Netherlands. www.olgamecking.com

Urdu Mom: A blog by Tamania Jaffri about her Pakistani/Canadian family raising their kids bilingually with Urdu/English in Canada. www.urdumom.com

ABOUT THE AUTHOR

Mariam Navaid Ottimofiore is a Pakistani expat author, writer, researcher and economist. When she was 19 years old, she left her home in Karachi with a blue suitcase and a one-way ticket to Boston. She has lived in nine countries as an expat child and an expat adult: The Kingdom of Bahrain, the United States, Pakistan, the United Kingdom, Germany, Denmark, Singapore, the United Arab Emirates and Ghana. 17 years and four continents later, her life on the move as an ATCK is messy. A 40-foot container, an expat husband from another corner of the world and two children born 3,000 miles apart have added complexity, challenges and many joys to living a multicultural, multilingual and multi-mobile life. She currently lives in Accra, Ghana, with her German/Italian husband and her German-Pakistani-Italian kids, born in Singapore and Dubai. Passionate about languages and cultures, Mariam speaks fluent Urdu, English, Hindi and German with some Italian, Danish and Arabic on the side. She is an expert at making embarrassing mistakes in every new language she picks up, is perpetually lost in every new city she calls home and can never remember her new address or where she packed those suede boots!

Mariam has a Bachelor of Arts degree in Economics and Political Science from Mount Holyoke College in the US and specialized in Economic Development at the University of Sussex in the UK. Her corporate career saw her work at Morgan Stanley in Houston, USA and Maersk Oil Trading, A.P Moller Maersk in Copenhagen, Denmark.

Mariam made a career change to a full-time writer in 2012. She is the co-author of two books *Export Success and Industrial Linkages in South Asia* (Palgrave Macmillan 2009) and *Insights and Interviews from the 2017 Families in Global Transition Conference* (Summertime Publishing 2018). She has been the Content Editor for *Fuchsia Magazine* in Singapore, and her expat writing has been published in *Expat Connect Dubai, Global Living Magazine, Expat Living Singapore, Expat Living Hong Kong, The Huffington Post, Sassy Mama Dubai,* Multicultural Kid Blogs and FIDI Global Relocation. Her expat life has been featured on the Oprah Winfrey Network (OWN) for Super Soul Sunday and her expat blog 'And Then We Moved To' has been shortlisted for 'Best Parent Blog 2017' by *Time Out Dubai Kids.* She has also been a conference speaker at the Families in Global Transition conference in The Hague in 2017 and 2018.

Photo courtesy of Leticia Gaidon Bradford Photography

WOULD YOU LIKE TO WORK WITH MARIAM?

If you would like to work with Mariam, you can hire her:

- As a contributing writer for your magazine (physical or online)
- As a content writer for your website if related to living abroad and/or expat life
- As a speaker on expat life and raising a globally mobile family
- As a workshop trainer on 'How to Build Your MOLA Family'
- As a podcast or interviewee expert on expat topics
- As a book club author to give a talk to your book club (online or offline)

You can contact Mariam at:

www.andthenwemovedto.com

mariamottimofiore@gmail.com

f /andthenwemovedto

𝕏 @andthenwemoved2

◎ @andthenwemovedto

in linkedin.com/in/mariamottimofiore

Also from Springtime Books and Summertime Publishing

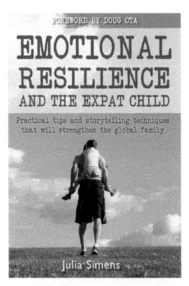

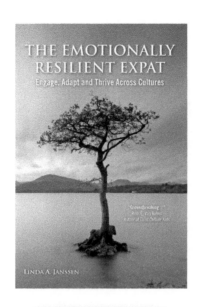

THE EMOTIONALLY RESILIENT EXPAT

Engage, Adapt and Thrive Across Cultures

"Groundbreaking..."
—Ruth E. Van Reken
Author of Third Culture Kids

LINDA A. JANSSEN

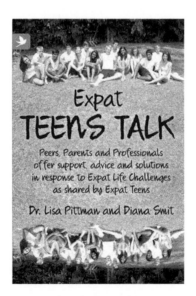

Expat TEENS TALK

Peers, Parents and Professionals
offer support, advice and solutions
in response to Expat Life Challenges
as shared by Expat Teens

Dr. Lisa Pittman and Diana Smit

Insights and interviews from
THE 2017 FAMILIES IN GLOBAL TRANSITION (FIGT) CONFERENCE

BUILDING ON THE BASICS:
CREATING YOUR TRIBE ON THE MOVE

Written By: Tone Delin Indrelid,
Jane Barron, Mariam Ottimofiore
and Sarah Janney Stoner with
Ginny Philps, Sarah Black, Carolyn
Parse Rizzo and Sara Coggiola

Edited by: Dounia Bertuccelli

AN
INCONVENIENT POSTING

AN EXPAT WIFE'S MEMOIR OF LOST IDENTITY

STATE OF TEXAS
EXPIRES
27 JULY

Laura J Stephens

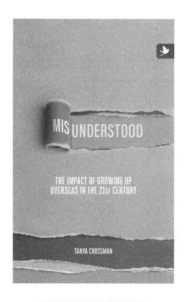

SLURPING SOUP
and other confusions:

true stories and activities to help
third culture kids during transition

"A much-needed resource." *Barry Dequanne, Head of School, American School of Brasilia*

SUNSHINE
SOUP
NOURISHING THE GLOBAL SOUL

Jo Parfitt

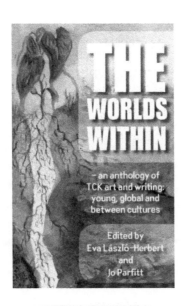

THE WORLDS WITHIN

– an anthology of
TCK art and writing:
young, global and
between cultures

Edited by
Eva László-Herbert
and
Jo Parfitt

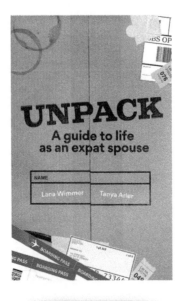

UNPACK
A guide to life
as an expat spouse

NAME

Lana Wimmer   Tanya Arler